PRENTICE-HALL FOUNDATIONS OF EDUCATION SERIES

Hobert W. Burns, Editor

A Social History of Education	Robert Holmes Beck
Problems in Education and Philosophy	Charles J. Brauner and Hobert W. Burns
Teaching and Learning: A Psychological Perspective	Thomas E. Clayton
Schools, Scholars, and Society	Jean Dresden Grambs
Tradition and Change in Education: A Comparative Study	Andreas M. Kazamias and Byron G. Massialas

A SOCIAL HISTORY OF EDUCATION

FOUNDATIONS OF EDUCATION SERIES

ROBERT HOLMES BECK

PRENTICE-HALL, INC., ENGLEWOOD CLIFFS, N. J.

A SOCIAL HISTORY
OF EDUCATION

PRENTICE-HALL INTERNATIONAL, INC., *London*
PRENTICE-HALL OF AUSTRALIA, PTY., LTD., *Sydney*
PRENTICE-HALL OF CANADA, LTD., *Toronto*
PRENTICE-HALL OF INDIA (PRIVATE) LTD., *New Delhi*
PRENTICE-HALL OF JAPAN, INC., *Tokyo*
PRENTICE-HALL DE MEXICO, S.A., *Mexico City*

TO MAEVE

FOUNDATIONS OF EDUCATION SERIES

A SOCIAL HISTORY OF EDUCATION
BY ROBERT HOLMES BECK

© COPYRIGHT 1965 BY PRENTICE-HALL, INC.
ENGLEWOOD CLIFFS, N. J.

Library of Congress
Catalog Card No.: 64-10849

PRINTED IN THE UNITED STATES OF AMERICA
C–81570-c   C–81569-p

Public education is the "growth industry" of the nation today.
Next to defense, education is the single largest enterprise in our
political economy and, unlike even defense, it is the one American
activity that in some way or at some time directly involves
every single citizen.

If public education is quantitatively important, then the training
of teachers is one of the most qualitatively important undertakings
of the entire educational enterprise. Indeed, the training of
teachers is already the single largest undertaking of American higher
education, since more college graduates enter the profession of
teaching than any other vocation, and it may well be the most
important undertaking of our colleges and universities.

Even so, despite the size of the American educational establishment,
it is remarkable how little is understood of the educative process,
especially of the intellectual bases of education that support all
pedagogy; and of all those who have—in the language of defense
rather than education—a "need to know," the prospective
teacher has the greatest need.

Prospective teachers need to understand education through the
historical perspective of Western culture—and so the series includes
a volume in the history of education, a volume that may fairly be
called an intellectual history of education, rather than a mere chronology
of educationally important dates or historically important pedagogues.

Prospective teachers need to understand that the school, and the
children and teachers in it, are social organisms inevitably influenced
by the nature of the society in which they exist—and so the series
includes a volume in the sociology of education, a volume showing
how the public school reflects, for better or worse, the reality
rather than the image of contemporary American society.

Prospective teachers need to understand the psychological nature of
children and how it limits, if not determines, what schools should
or should not do (Is it reasonable to expect, as many teachers do,
a six- or seven-year-old to sit quietly and attentively for a major portion
of his waking day?)—and so the series includes a volume in the psychology
of education, a volume that pays particular attention to the ways in
which children grow, develop, mature, learn, and change their behavior.

FOUNDATIONS OF EDUCATION SERIES

Prospective teachers need to understand the close functional relationship between philosophy and practice in education and, at the same time, to see that many of the practical problems they will face as teachers (e.g., How shall I grade? Shall I use drill? Should children be segregated on such bases as talent, color, or religion?) are solvable only in terms of prior philosophic inquiry—and so the series includes a volume in philosophy of education, a volume that views philosophy as dressed in the working clothes of a practical discipline rather than in the former attire of impractical abstractions.

Prospective teachers need perspective to see the historical, philosophical, social, and psychological foundations of education in a context both different and larger than any one locality, region, or nation affords—and so the series includes a volume in comparative education, a volume designed to help the teacher compare and contrast his experience and educational system with the experiences and systems of other teachers in other nations and cultures.

These things the prospective teacher needs to know; he needs to be well grounded in the foundations of education, for they represent the intellectual tools that can give him scholarly leverage in his profession. But, given the thinness of time and the immensity of need in teacher education curriculums, how is this to be done?

The authors of this series believe that no single volume, be it a large, well-edited book of readings or a long treatise by one scholar, can meet the challenge of offering prospective teachers what they need to know as well as can a series of smaller volumes, each written by a specialist in one particular aspect of the foundations of education. Each volume in this series, by design, can stand alone as an introduction to an intellectual discipline; but when taken together the volumes unite these independent yet related disciplines into a series that offers prospective teachers a fuller, more unified introduction to the subject matters that underlie the profession of teaching.

We are convinced that prospective teachers who study these volumes in the foundations of education, and who discuss the concepts and issues presented with their instructors, will take to their future classrooms a firmer understanding not only of how to do the teaching job at hand but, more significant, of why their teaching job is so surpassingly important.

Hobert W. Burns

CONTENTS

History is a record—but not a photographic record—of events and relationships exactly as they were. The historian interprets this record, hopefully, with accuracy. In history, events do not speak for themselves; their meaning must be determined by the historian. The task of interpreting history is subtle; its pitfalls are hinted at by E. H. Dance in the title of his *History the Betrayer: A Study in Bias* (2).[1] Gross bias can be guarded against in this task; it is the innocent bias that is so difficult to limit. For example, historians of ancient Greece are prone to see Athens during the fourth and fifth centuries B.C. as a "factory," producing the best that Western civilization has ever produced, intellectually and even aesthetically. They exaggerate, but cannot be said to mislead, to falsify.

One of the more common interpretations of educational history is utilitarian, interpreting the history of education in response to the needs and opportunities of the day. Perhaps the oldest systematic history of education was written

[1] Numbers in parentheses refer to selections in the bibliography at the end of each chapter.

1

INTRODUCTION

1

with a utilitarian mode of interpretation, Abbé Claude Fleury's *Traité du choix et de la méthode des études* (*Treatise on the Selection and Method of Studies*), which H. G. Good identifies as the first systematic history of education (3). Fleury, who lived from 1640 until 1723, came to such a typically utilitarian conclusion as: that Roman education was crowned by the training of "orators," trial attorneys, because Rome had a need for such men. Utilitarianism is an appealing form of interpretation. Distinguished men have used it, among them the nineteenth century English philosopher, Herbert Spencer, whose utilitarianism in writing on education appeared in the essay "What Knowledge Is of Most Worth?" (1859).

Although utilitarianism has proved useful in interpreting history of education, it will not be the governing type of interpretation in this book, for the utilitarian does not explain enough. Comprehensiveness of explanation, after all, is one of the criteria in assessing the adequacy of a theory. In weighing utilitarianism, it is clear that the theory has to be stretched pretty far to explain the vigor with which so many educators have denounced vocational and specialized training, or so hotly championed "liberal" and "general" education, schooling intended to further the end of self-realization.

What follows will propose certain revisions in conventional, standard interpretations of education. Fair treatment of events, ideas, and relationships will be the end sought. From time to time, objection will be registered to an interpretation that seems to have been unfair. One case in point is the fate of the Elder Sophists in ancient Greece. Another example is the disparagement of the five centuries that followed the traditional date of the fall of Rome, A.D. 476. These centuries conventionally are labelled "the Dark Ages." In Chapter 2, the Elder Sophists will have their contribution to social and political thought appraised, with a view to weighing its implications for education. In the same spirit of revision for the sake of fairer treatment, Chapter 3 will argue that the so-called Dark Ages be thought of as a period of transition.

Perhaps the most venturesome revision will be that undertaken with respect to Plato. The heart of the approach will be the assertion that Plato's influence in the history of education came through his *social and political philosophy*. The conventional treatment of Plato in histories of education stresses his theory of ideas, but not his social and political philosophy. It was the latter that held startling implications for the aims of education, the extent of educational opportunity, and the most worthwhile studies in school.

Later chapters will present other revisions. The role of the liberal arts faculty of the University of Paris in the fourteenth century, fighting for "academic freedom," will be proposed as one of the most important contributions of the medieval universities. This fight for academic freedom was a stirring series of episodes.

Of great magnitude among influences tempering the course of educational history has been the science of education. It is difficult to understand why histories of education have spent so little time on the history of the science of education, for nothing has become more important in shaping the process of modern teaching. This book will attempt to revise the historical position of educational science.

The very nature of history-making permits, even invites, revisionism. History is the record generally agreed upon by record-makers. Any serious student of the records is professionally obligated to voice his judgment on the interpretations that have been made. Some interpretations stand for quite a time, and the case they make seems open and shut. In time, however, even these histories strike some students as less than comprehensive; omissions and oversimplification appear.

Revisionism, then, is not new in the telling of history. The classic case of revision is the reassessment of the "frontier hypothesis" of Frederick Jackson Turner. What happened to men and women who lived on a frontier intrigued Turner and made him feel that frontier life had made America distinctive from Europe. Turner advanced this in 1893 (8), and it quickly became *the* view of American history and remained so until the 1930's. Historians of the American scene were caught up in Turner's vision of how the United States had been molded by its vast reaches of free land, the steady settlement of that land, and the western migration.

When Turner died in 1932, there were several serious challenges to his frontier hypothesis. Critics, with more or less justification, charged that Turner had neglected the influences of social classes, urbanization, and industrialization. Turner's ironclad interpretation was seen to be vulnerable (1). It must always be so with the writing of history.

PROMETHEAN HUMANISM

Though neither utilitarianism nor any other doctrinaire interpretation consciously will direct this study, a viewpoint has recommended itself. Study of the difference in social-political philosophy distinguishing the conservatism of Plato from the liberalism [2] of the Elder Sophists has led to the formulation of this viewpoint, which will be titled *Promethean humanism*, a liberal social, political, and educational outlook.

Prometheus is remembered as a Titan who helped Zeus become chief of the gods. In return for his aid, Prometheus petitioned Zeus to set aside his plan to destroy mankind. The gesture symbolized Prometheus' love of mankind (*philanthropia*), as later did his stealing of fire (science-technology) and giving it to man, for which he was punished by being crucified.

[2] The liberal tradition in the history of education is the tradition of those who pressed for an extension of educational opportunity to the lower classes, a broadening of the course of study, and a recognition of people and studies, including science and vocational education, to which the conservative tradition has been cool.

The full meaning of the term *Promethean humanism* cannot be spelled out at once, but its essence can be felt in *Prometheus Bound*, the lyric drama of Aeschylus, first performed in Athens between 473-63 B.C. For centuries, the liberal spirit awakened by the Elder Sophists and by Aeschylus lay quiescent, buried by the conservatism of Plato and Aristotle. In the Enlightenment it was revived, and can be seen in the *Prometheus Unbound* of Shelley, or in the poems on Promethean themes by Byron and Goethe. Anyone whose sympathies are captured by the Promethean will be indebted to Eric A. Havelock and his *The Crucifixion of Intellectual Man* (4), as well as his *The Liberal Temper in Greek Politics* (5). In the dramas of Aeschylus and Shelley, Zeus represents Power, including the power to destroy mankind. In *Prometheus Bound* Aeschylus portrays Prometheus as a symbol of love for mankind and confidence in man and in the free use of his educated intelligence. The liberalism Aeschylus endorses might be called Promethean because of the belief that many men, and not just a few, can be educated to be inclined to intelligence and humane behavior. This point of view is compatible with democracy but not with aristocracy, with liberty, but not with authoritarianism.

The conservative tradition is not Promethean. If mythology were to be tapped for the conservative hero, that figure might be the brother of Prometheus, Epimetheus. As the name *Prometheus* means "forethought," the name *Epimetheus* denotes "thought of what has gone before."

The conservative vision of the world tends to present contemporary conditions as much less attractive than they were presumed to have been during a golden age. Of course, the specific qualities of golden ages have varied over the centuries, but a few basic qualities have endured. The conservatives have always preferred a state of affairs in which there is a minimum of change, instability, and adventure. Since the time of Plato, conservatives have assumed that society would be stable and orderly if it were ruled by an aristocracy, hopefully an intellectual aristocracy. But all aristocracies that have arisen since have been hereditary and not intellectual. Nevertheless, conservatives have preferred aristocracy to democracy.

In this preference for stability, aristocratic-conservative thinkers have not favored the growing influence of science and technology, industrialization, urbanization, or a high degree of social and physical mobility; these all have threatened to promote and have promoted change. For this reason, the French and American Revolutions were equally repugnant to that model conservative, Edmund Burke (1729-97), who wrote *Reflections on the Revolution in France* (6), the classic conservative rebuke to all social and political change that proceeds at more than a snail's pace. Burke's *Reflections* reveals the conservative mind at its best.

The differences between the conservative and liberal traditions are almost predictable when each is concerned with aims of education, extent of educational opportunity, and curricular contents. Conservatives, starting with Plato, have urged education mostly for those whom they believed ought to lead society. For these future leaders the conservatives have never suggested vocational education or even education in sciences. The chosen educational fare has been the humanities, subjects such as history and literature, in which the future leaders could see models for their own behavior. The models were traditional paradigms; the view again was backward in time toward the golden ages, when true heroes were assumed to have lived on earth. The ancient Greeks thus offered Homer's *Iliad* to their future leaders when the latter were boys, expecting large sections of the *Iliad* to be committed to memory.

In the liberal way of thinking, education has always had more of a Promethean flavor. Again, in early Greece, at the time when young men of Athens could take advantage of new opportunities in commerce, government, and science, the Sophists, who were liberals, arose to teach competence in all these areas. This manner of thinking is quite reminiscent of Abbé Fleury, who thought that subjects of study were born of social needs and opportunities.

Benjamin Franklin was a liberal, but a Promethean in education, not just because he insisted on the schools offering subjects that practiced young Americans in the skills the country then could use. Historians of education have referred to Franklin's "realism"; Franklin has been described as a realist, as opposed to a humanist. In general, the liberals have sided with realism—practical and scientific studies—against humanism. But the polarity can be mischievously exaggerated. The fact of the matter is that the distinction between the two has been one of emphasis. Historically, conservatives, aristocrats, and humanists have been suspicious of the practice of science when it has been sought as a way of controlling nature, increasing the standard of living, increasing a nation's power—of promoting change. On the other hand, liberals and realists have scoffed at the humanists as backward-looking, selfish, timid, and indifferent to human welfare.

These were the suspicions that defined the "two cultures" to which C. P. Snow drew attention in his *The Two Cultures and the Scientific Revolution* (7). One culture was presumed by Snow to have been inhabited by men of science, the other by men of letters. The education that appealed to the former was supposed to be realistic; the latter, the humanists, were expected to elect humanities. As Snow himself has insisted, the thought of the two cultures at odds is intolerable. Science and technology do not deny art any more than art or any of the humanities denies science. The two cultures have developed, not because it was only logical that they should, but because of the success Plato met in his division of the pure from the applied, the theoretical from the practical, of those who determine policy and make decisions from those who work and fight for the state.

Before Plato's influence overthrew the Sophists and became the chief influence in the Western world, the Greeks had seen the pure and the applied

5

combined in a single concept, *techne* or craft, which comprehended both statecraft and handicraft. In a way, this book is meant to reinforce the old Greek idea of *techne*. This reinforcement, in a way, expresses agreement with the modern endeavor to reconcile the two cultures of the humanities and science (and within science, of pure science with technology). But the thrust at reconciliation is pre-Platonic, and for that reason we recall the symbolism of Prometheus in Aeschylus' drama, choosing to identify as *Promethean humanism* the philosophy of education that influences our historical interpretation.

Promethean humanism allies both science and the humanities. Prometheus spoke for both, for human intelligence understood as science—technology—and as human sensibility, expressed in the feelings of men, and even in their art and their love.

Promethean humanism reaches out to both liberalism and conservatism, at least to the conservative who is aware of certain traditions, one who demands liberty for men and esteems the ideal of equality of opportunity. For Aeschylus, as for Shelley, Prometheus was not a revolutionary or anarchistic figure. In the dramas of both poets, Prometheus was crucified by Zeus but did not hate his tormentor. In fact, Prometheus thought ahead to his ultimate reconciliation with Zeus, to the reconciliation of Intelligence-Philanthropy with Power, a reconciliation absolutely necessary for the survival of humanity. Promethean humanism, then, is offered as a modern remedy, but a very old formula.

BIBLIOGRAPHY

1. BILLINGTON, RAY A., *The American Frontier: Service Center for Teachers of History*. Washington, D.C.: American Historical Association, 1958.

2. DANCE, E. H., *History the Betrayer: A Study in Bias*. London: Hutchinson & Co., Ltd., 1960.

3. GOOD, H. G., "Rise of the History of Education," *History of Education Journal*, VIII, No. 3 (1957), 81-85.

4. HAVELOCK, E. A., *The Crucifixion of Intellectual Man*. Boston: Beacon Press, Inc., 1950.

5. ———, *The Liberal Temper in Greek Politics*. New Haven: Yale University Press, 1957.

6. MAHONEY, THOMAS H. D., ed., *Edmund Burke: Reflections on the Revolution in France*. New York: The Liberal Arts Press, 1955.

7. SNOW, C. P., *The Two Cultures and the Scientific Revolution*. New York: Cambridge University Press, 1959.

8. TURNER, FREDERICK JACKSON, *The Frontier in American History*. New York: Holt, Rinehart & Winston, Inc., 1940.

Students interested in the discussions on the role of the history of education in the professional preparation of teachers are referred to the *History of Education Journal*, Vol. VII, Numbers 1, 2, and 3 (1955-56). These issues of the *Journal* carry the full reports of the Committee on Historical Foundations of the National Society of College Teachers of Education.

Education goes further into the past than extant historical records trace. The Old Stone Age man, most familiar to us, who lived during the Acheulean period, between 300,000 and 75,000 B.C., evolved a variety of tools: cleavers, knives, scrapers, picks, and choppers. But he was not the first user of tools. Pre-Chellean men, living more than a million years ago, had invented hammers, cores, and edged flakes. The Leakeys, digging in the Olduvai Gorge of Tanganyika, East Africa, found tools that may date back 1,750,000 years (16).

Were these toolmakers taught or did they simply imitate? (10) Judging from the educational activities of the New Stone Age, the neolithic tribes alive today, there is good reason to believe that teaching was at least as prevalent as imitation. Many kinds of skills, attitudes, knowledge (of kinship relations, for example) have been thought too complicated for mastery by unsupervised imitation. Also, some preliterate groups actually have had schools, as the "bush" schools of East and West Africa with their buildings and specialized staff (22).

7

EDUCATION IN ANCIENT GREECE AND ROME

2

At least a thousand years before the earliest Greek peoples learned to read and write, both of these arts had become conspicuous in the culture of the Harappan civilization in the Indus Valley of what today is Pakistan. Equally as old, or older, were the scribe or writing cultures of Mesopotamia, between the Tigris and Euphrates Rivers (1, 4, 13, 20). In that fertile triangle lived the Sumerians, succeeded by the Babylonians, who, in their turn, were overpowered by the Assyrians. In Egypt there were scribes as early as 3500 B.C., twenty-five centuries before the Bronze Age of which Homer wrote in the *Iliad* and *Odyssey*. Nor were these civilizations limited to the elements of reading and writing. In literature, mathematics, astronomy, commerce, and religion each arrived at high levels of sophistication. They had schools, some of which were private, while others operated in temples and palaces.

Neolithic culture, the ancestor to antique Greek civilization, developed between 3000 and 1000 B.C. The island of Crete saw the oldest Aegean settlements of peoples who had migrated from Asia Minor (14), but little is known of the first centuries of Greek history. After 800 B.C., however, historic evidence becomes more plentiful and it is possible to refer to a Hellenic civilization, lasting roughly from 800-338 B.C. The latter date marks the battle of Chaeronea, won by King Philip of the Greek state of Macedon, who forced all the separate Greek city-states into an "empire," opening the Hellenistic Age which lasted till A.D. 529, when the Christian emperor Justinian promulgated an order closing the "pagan schools."

In the latter half of the Hellenistic period, the greatest system of education known to antiquity developed. One of the crowning features was the "University of Athens" (a congery of the Academy started by Plato, the Lyceum of Aristotle, the school of Zeno the Stoic, and that of Epicurus, founder of Epicureanism). There were facilities for advanced education throughout the Hellenistic world—in Antioch, Smyrna, Rhodes, Cos, Nicaea, Nocmedia, Pella, Pergamus, Soli, and Tarsus. The Romans Cicero, his brother, Marcus, as well as the poets Horace and Ovid studied at Athens. Caesar and Brutus were both scholars at Rhodes. Ascendant above all Hellenistic educational achievements was the vast library at Alexandria, Egypt, then part of the Hellenistic Empire (21). For seven hundred years the library and a "museum," where scholars could live, played host to the most formidable intellectual group that was to be gathered in any one place till most recent times. By the first century B.C. the holdings of the library totalled some 700,000 manuscripts, and by A.D. 646, when Alexandria was captured by the Muslim troops of Amr ibn al-As, who fed the manuscripts to the furnaces heating the baths of Alexandria, there may have been a million manuscripts.

The magnitude of the loss becomes apparent not only when one realizes that at the time of the destruction the library may have had a million manuscripts, but also when one remembers that most of the greatest scholars of the Hellenistic world at one time or another were engaged in research at Alexandria, such men as the geometrician Euclid, and the physicists Archimedes, Hero, and Philo. The *Almagest*, an Arabic adaptation of Claudius Ptolemy's *Syntaxis*, was published at the library and became the basis for the geocentric theory of the universe, a theory that was accepted without challenge throughout the Middle Ages until the sixteenth century, when Copernicus presented the first serious criticism of it. Nor were scientists the only pride of Alexandria. The fourth director of the library, Aristarchus, established the study of grammar. The cultural richness of Alexandria indicates the dominance Greece attained over the ancient Western world.

What was the Hellenic and Hellenistic formula for education that proved so potent? (18) The classic Hellenic-Hellenistic prescription, as preached if not practiced, combined the idea and ideal of excellence in character or will (morals), physique (body), and mind (reason). This provided the first meaning of the term *humanism*. To a humanist, human beings were capable of being trained to excellence in body, mind, and character.

Perhaps it would be more accurate to describe this philosophy of education as Athenian, for it was evolved by men who came to teach in Athens. In Sparta, the only city that rivalled Athens, the ideal was education that had patriotism as its objective, education that emphasized body-building and games preparatory for war.

It is not quite accurate to suggest that the Athenian philosophy of education finally decided on a balance of mind, character, and body. Concern for intellectual matters was brought about by a group known as Sophists, and really did not catch on till later in the fifth century, or, perhaps, until the fourth century—the time of Plato, Isocrates, and Aristotle. In earlier centuries the stress of educators had been on the development of character and physique, a view of education created by Homer.

THE HOMERIC PHILOSOPHY OF EDUCATION

The blind poet Homer lived in the eighth or ninth century B.C. His epic poems, the *Iliad* and the *Odyssey*, describe twelfth century Mycenaean civilization. Homer's importance for education lies in the fact that the virtues and ideals praised in his epic poems were accepted as the goals for Greek education (7), even as late as the fifth and fourth centuries B.C. In those sophisticated times, the Homeric philosophy of education was not displaced, but simply supplemented for a *secondary* school level by mathematical studies (as recommended by Plato), and by grammar and rhetoric,

9

urged by the Elder or Rhetorical Sophists, of whom Isocrates (436-338 B.C.) was the most famous (19).

For the instruction of youth between the ages of seven and fourteen, the Homeric ideals, the athletic games, the chant of epic poems by boys accompanying themselves on the lyre, seem never to have lost their appeal for the ancient Greeks. Though in Hellenistic days children were expected to learn the three R's, more conservative Athenians looked wistfully to Sparta, where the Homeric tradition continued almost unadulterated. These Athenians regretted what they said was the loss of attention to the Homeric virtues of personal courage, loyalty, and reverence for the gods. One has only to read Aristophanes' comedy, *The Clouds* (3), to sense conservative disappointment with curricular changes that added oratorical training and philosophy to the education of Athenian youth. Nor did the claims that training in oratory would also teach a great deal of subject matter other than simply how to speak effectively help mitigate conservative disappointment. Aristophanes, and those who agreed with him that Homer's values, plus gymnastics and learning to play the lyre as accompaniment to Homeric verse, could supply all that a young man needed to learn at school, were quite impatient with the Sophists' introduction of subtle discussions of morality and politics into the curriculum. The conservatives scorned the ideal of the "polymath," a man of "general education," well-schooled in many subjects. "Let men be virtuous, courageous, and strong," they said, "and sophistication will not be needed."

Looking carefully at Homer's *Iliad* (the *Odyssey* being less influential in ancient and classic Greek education), the historian finds not only the recommendation of an entire curriculum; Homer even supplied model teachers, Phoenix and Chiron, who, he said, had taught Achilles. From Chiron Achilles had learned to hunt, ride horseback, throw a javelin, and the courtly art of playing the lyre. Phoenix was charged by King Peleus, father of Achilles, to teach Achilles "to give good counsel and how to perform great deeds" (18). Since Homer was describing life in a feudal society of warrior-nobles, grouped about a king and living in a patriarchal society, what he had Phoenix and Chiron teach Achilles was exactly what the feudal noble had to know, in *both* ancient Greek times and in the much later period of feudalism in western Europe.

Because European aristocracies later found the Homeric model so attractive, it is worth reflecting on some of the suppositions Homer took for granted. (One was that most men could not be educated.) As an aristocrat, Plato was to say in the *Meno*, "virtue cannot be taught." By this he must have meant that a boy has to be born in an aristocratic family to be of a type who would have natural virtue and be able to cultivate it. As Aristotle was to put it four hundred years later: some men are born to be slaves. The aristocratic poet, Pindar, joined the poet Theognis in urging that education be limited to those who were born "good men." Wrote Pindar: "Be the kind

of man you know yourself to be." That is to say: education will polish and ✗
exercise native virtues and talents. This point of view fitted well into an
aristocratic and conservative social philosophy that maintained that some
men are born to govern, and others to work and be ruled.

No mention has been made of the schooling of women. Although not all
Hellenes came to agree with Aristotle that women are subject to the will
of men, almost as slaves, Hellenic society remained patriarchal. Penelope,
the faithful stay-at-home wife of Ulysses described by Homer in the *Odyssey*,
was the model for young women. It was enough for a woman to learn to
manage a household and to educate the very young.

THE ELDER SOPHISTS

By the fifth century B.C., time had run out for the land-owning aristocracy,
the *eupatrids*. This was certainly so in Athens. In 462-61, two Athenians,
Ephialtes and Pericles, won support for a political reform that ended the
power of the *Areopagus*, the supreme judiciary, whose membership once
had been exclusively aristocratic. Little by little, that aristocratic monopoly
of legislative power had been eroded. A hundred years earlier the chief administrator (*archon*) of Athens was Solon, appointed in 594 or 595. While
Solon preserved a large measure of political, and, particularly, judicial
power in aristocratic hands (on the assumption that aristocrats had been
educated to exercise responsible leadership), he enlarged the power of small
landowners (*georgi*) and artisans (*demiurgi*). Both of the latter won ad-
mittance to the Assembly. Moreover, Solon guaranteed freedom of the person; Athenians could be enslaved for debt and all were to be equal before
the law, whereas formerly the aristocracy controlled the courts as well as
the legislature.

What Solon began at the opening of the century, Clisthenes continued
in the last decade of the century. The political power of the lower classes
was enhanced.

The trend toward political democracy, coupled with a growing respect
for sea-borne commerce, business, and handicrafts, was to have significant
consequences for Hellenic educational theory. By 461, Pericles and Ephialtes had ended the power of the Areopagus, the only powerful Greek city-
state having aristocratic control being Sparta. Sparta then became the ideal
of the Athenian Right Wing, the devotees of Homer, the conservative aristocrats who had lost their grip at home. In Athens, the Council of 500 and
the popularly dominated Assembly controlled all legislation, not only under
Pericles but for a long time thereafter. The Athenian constitution became
truly democratic, with direct government by the majority of the people; by
457, even the poorest citizen could stand for election. Property qualifications, both for voting and for holding office, had been abolished.

Paralleling the increase in the political rights and strength of the lower
orders in Athenian society was an increase in wealth for all classes, particu-

11

larly the artisan group. For two hundred years after Homer's death, no grave threat from overseas was posed to the Hellenes. The Greek islands sent colonizers abroad, principally to southern Italy and Sicily. Colonies in these areas were to play an important part in the Hellenization of Rome, although their ostensible purposes were to house surplus population, to find raw materials to be used in the mother country, and to establish markets. When Solon became Archon of Athens, he not only continued to sponsor colonization but took an active part in promoting commerce. Traders and artisans were invited to take up residence in Athens until there came to be over 45,000 resident aliens in the city.

Athenian currency was reformed, making it easier to trade with. When Solon retired, the artisans, what today would be called the lower middle class, were making money and enjoying the increase in freedom and political responsibility. While they did not sit on the Areopagus, they did have a say in elections and in setting the agenda of the legislative Assembly. None of these new rights were they willing to forego, and the so-called tyranny of Peisistratus and his sons (546-510) found Peisistratus and his successors taking property from the aristocracy, exiling the less docile of the aristocrats, and enriching the artisans. Cleisthenes, who came to power at the end of the fifth century, ensured that the happy state of affairs for the "commoners" would not be ended.

Fortunately for Athens, the threats of Persian Kings Darius and Xerxes, which came at the turn of the century, were successfully met in a series of memorable campaigns, two of whose great battles were Marathon and Salamis. By 465, and certainly by 462, the Persian menace was extinguished for a century. Athens emerged from the Persian wars a powerful, as well as a rich, city-state. Holding the treasury of what was known as the Confederacy of Delos, of the Ionian States, Athens, not quite honestly, enriched herself and dominated Aegean trade.

The spread of democracy, which meant that many could be influential in government, paved the way for teachers of rhetoric and oratory. These teachers were the Elder or Rhetorical Sophists, who offered to prepare young men for the new opportunities that presented themselves in Athens. To the old guard, these sophistic teachers seemed little more than money-makers who would fashion youth after their own image. The conservatives, including Plato, disliked the thought of young men studying to be influential and wealthy, rather than studying to cultivate the body, mind, and character. The dichotomy was clearly between the conservative-aristocrats, inclined to the Homeric virtues—and in the instance of Plato, to a life of philosophic inquiry—and the Sophists, who were interested in learning about the world of nature and man in the hope of learning to manage both. But it is not to be supposed that the Sophists, with rare exceptions, were indifferent to the morality of the young men they taught. One has only to read Isocrates (19), or the Roman Cicero (23), to sense the moral idealism of the Sophists. They were not teaching young men only how to become rich and powerful; the sophistic objective was rather to help students grow in sophistication and effectiveness as citizens bent on improving the lot of man.

The Sophists were teachers who exactly fitted Abbé Fleury's later utilitarian interpretation of the history of education. As was mentioned above, Fleury advanced the idea that educational innovations are in response to the "needs" of the times. Most simply described, the Sophists were intellectuals (*sophistes*) attracted to Athens from all corners of ancient Hellas (9). The best-known Sophists taught in the last half of the fifth century and throughout the fourth century B.C.; they were five or six in number, but the dates of birth and death of even the most famous are uncertain. There is good reason to believe that Gorgias of Leotini lived from about 485-380, and that Protagoras of Addira, Hippias, and Prodicus lived at approximately the same time. We know little of the Sophists, basically because Plato (427-348 B.C.) thoroughly denigrated Sophism in a series of dialogues, the *Sophist*, the *Hippias*, the *Gorgias*, the *Republic*, *Protagoras*, *Meno*, and the *Phaedrus*. So great did Plato's reputation become that the Western world came to accept his judgment of the Elder Sophists and to lose interest in sophistic writings (9).

There were two sophistic curriculums, just as there were two groups of Sophists. One was based on natural science and the other, more influential, on rhetoric and political science. At least one Sophist, Democritus (*c*.460-370 B.C.), taught both natural and political science, but the emphasis of Empedocles (identified with Democritus in early speculation on an atomic view of physical structures), Heraclitus, and Parmenides was on physical science. These men are prominent in the history of science and philosophy, but they only affected higher education as it appeared in the late Hellenistic universities.

The chief influence of the Sophists was on secondary education, to which they introduced the study of grammar and rhetoric after the fifth century. This was their foremost educational achievement, and one that has lasted till modern times. The success of the Elder Sophists, despite Plato's attack on them, was indeed that they met what many sensed to be the needs of the time.

The fact that the Sophists charged high fees meant that the instruction was for the aristocratic youth, despite any sophistic interest in democracy. Protagoras was said to have charged 10,000 drachmas for a two- or three-year course at a time when a drachma was a skilled worker's daily wage. By 350, however, the price of such a course of study had fallen to about 1,000 drachmas—there were more teachers available—and a few seemed willing to offer a course for as little as 300 drachmas. But even 300 drachmas was more than any worker, artisan, or small landowner could afford. And how the aristocrats mocked the Sophists, who made their living by teaching, for charging for instruction!

To Plato, all Sophists taught young men to ignore the justice of any particular case, seeking only to win an argument. Although some Sophists were open to this charge, they were denounced by other, reputable Sophists. The students of the leading Sophists were taught to fight for justice and to learn how a just cause might be identified. But for Plato, that teaching was in vain; virtue could not be taught. Only the "rich, the wise, and the well-born," as Plato's student, Aristotle, was later to describe the aristocrats, might be depended upon. In fact, Plato turned his back on the reform of the city-state (see the *Georgias*), preferring the cultivation of "the city he [the philosopher] bears within himself." Plato's ideal became more and more one of inner perfection that had nothing to do with sophistic, Promethean visions of progress that might be made in society.

In direct contrast with Plato, the Elder Sophists' view of anthropology held that society was evolving and could progress *if men learned to guide their affairs effectively*. Politics, democracy—the form of government in which the Rhetorical Sophists had such confidence—called for men able to point up relevant data in complex issues, men capable of stating all sides of the argument, able to help a group attain consensus in discussions leading to decisions.

Plato, declaring that thoughtful men find public life so disappointing that they must turn away and cultivate the life of mind and spirit, had much less interest than did the Sophists in helping the Athenians learn to make democracy work. Unlike the Sophists, he believed that men were born, destined for a low or a high social position, for subservience or for leadership. (Aristotle, it will be recalled [17], went beyond this and stated that some men are born to be slaves, by nature are intended to be slaves.) Moreover, he felt that society could be at peace only if the Golden Age that had earlier seen men living out their lives in the station to which their natures destined them were restored.

This reactionary social thought was not shared by the Sophists. For them, men were amiable by nature. By nature they were fitted for social living, but only education would permit them to learn the arts and crafts needed for success in living in a peaceful society. Moreover, the Sophists honored all the crafts, holding statecraft to be but one of them. Here, again, was a major distinction between sophistic and Platonic thought. Plato, the aristocrat, distinguished between the crafts and science-philosophy. From Plato, the Western world inherited the idea that craft or technology was unworthy of a gentleman, that training in craft had no place in a liberal education. The Sophists differed strongly with Plato on the value of *techne* (craft), but their voice was lost in later times; today, many parts of the world, in desperate need of technicians, find themselves saddled with a system of education, a legacy of Plato, that has no place for education in craft, not even in craft perceived as engineering. The words of Aeschylus have been lost, when in *Prometheus Bound* (8) the Titan Prometheus, lover of mankind, refers to himself as "the great resource that is technology." For Aeschylus science-technology (the Greeks made no distinction) had rescued mankind from savagery; mankind could progress by means of its intelligent use. But Prometheus was lost to the Western world as a symbol of human progress until the eighteenth century, when the myth was revived by the liberal poets of the Enlightenment. During the intervening centuries, at least until the sixteenth, it was uncommon to find a thoughtful person who was optimistic about possibilities for progress in the management of human affairs. The Sophists, scientists, and rhetoricians had just such optimism, such faith in the potentiality of men for intelligent, socially responsible self-rule, and dominion over nature. This optimism, this faith in mankind, is Promethean humanism; but it is naïve without the support of education. No liberal, no Promethean humanist—certainly not a Sophist—has ever believed that men could achieve what they potentially might without education.

The hopes of the Sophists, the Private Histories, were snuffed out by a combination of circumstances. Perhaps the worst blow came with the second Peloponnesian War (431-404 B.C.), which a strong Athens entered under the leadership of the great Promethean governor-general, Pericles. Pericles died in an epidemic when the war was but two years old, however, and the course he steered for Athens was scrapped in favor of a policy of faithless, self-defeating treatment of allies. Bitterness inevitably followed the defeat at the hands of Sparta. The Sophists were made scapegoats, and one of their most famous members, Socrates, executed on the spurious charge that he and his fellows had caused the ruin of the city by leading the youth from the traditional Homeric virtues and the old religion.

Coupled with this victimization came the attacks on Plato. Perhaps the Sophists could have survived even these, but Athens, indeed all the Hellenic city-states, had forgotten how to live at peace. Internecine war characterized the Hellenic world and was impossible to stop, even though Isocrates, the last of the great Rhetorical Sophists, led a movement of pan-Hellenism. He failed, however, and the Hellenic world he loved metamorphosed into the Hellenistic. The date of transition, 338 B.C., marked both the death of Isocrates and the battle of Chaeronea, at which Philip of Macedon won the right to unite ancient Greece in the Hellenistic, Alexandrian Empire, with the political and cultural capital Alexandria in Egypt, not Athens.

How shall the educational philosophy of Isocrates, whom the distinguished French historian Marrou dubs "the supreme master of oratorical culture" (18), be perceived with respect to that of Plato, the chief rival of Isocrates? It is probably best to perceive their views, not as antagonistic, but complementary. The one looked outward, hoping to school good men, skillful in the affairs of the citizen. Plato sought his objective in the cultivation of the "inner man." Is it thinkable that the two views can be held to be mutually exclusive, as the two poles of a magnet? Is not a good man concerned both with his personal excellence and the excellence of his effects on the world around him?

The fourth century B.C. was probably the most fruitful of the ancient Western world. This certainly is true for the historian of education, who finds Isocrates, Plato, and Aristotle all active in the first half of the century.

By the beginning of the fourth century the Elder Sophists were dead— Protagoras died in 421 and Prodicus in 399, only Gorgias living until 380. The liberal social-political philosophy was crushed, a fact symbolized by the growing influence of Plato's student and successor, Aristotle (384-321 B.C.). Like his teacher, Aristotle opened a school, the Lyceum, which had a continuous history till A.D. 529, when it was one of the pagan schools closed by Emperor Justinian. Some of the most influential intellectuals of the Hellenistic world either graduated from or taught at the Lyceum. There is good reason to believe that even the museum and library of Alexandria were molded along Aristotelian lines. The botanical, biological, mathematical, and astronomical studies of Alexandria exemplified the interests and the *research methods* pioneered by Aristotle. There was no branch of learning in which Aristotle did not work, and at a very high level, including literary criticism (the *Poetics*). It is little wonder that people of the later Middle Ages often titled Aristotle *Magister*, the master teacher, the judge in intellectual matters. St. Thomas referred to him with a single word, *Philosophus*, "the philosopher."

16

There is a very great deal for which Aristotle is to be remembered in the history of education: his attention to logic, other areas of philosophy, empirical science, rhetoric, and literary criticism, and his most conservative social-political philosophy. However, the Aristotelian contribution to education can perhaps be reduced to two major categories, one concerned with nature of knowledge and the means of attaining it, and the other involved with society and politics. Aristotle's writings on these topics are a wonderful mixture of original thought and marvelously organized reviews of the reflection of others. For his writings on the first major category, the student would have to read *Metaphysics* (17), the *Categories*, and the *Posterior Analytics*. In these three books are found Aristotle's views of the nature of reality, the relations between things, ideas, and events, and the possibilities of knowing. For what Aristotle believed was *known*, one would turn to *Physics*, *On the Heavens*, and *On the Soul*—a book on psychology.

In their way, the *Poetics* and Aristotle's writing on rhetoric are also excursions into the area of knowing. *Poetics* attempts to formulate criteria for judging literature and drama. Aristotle's thoughts on rhetoric sum up and improve upon the systematic work of Plato (on dialectic) and the rhetorical

Sophists. Perhaps Aristotle's thoughts on literary criticism and logic were his most original; even if not, the *Poetics* remains a standard work to this day, and all literary critics must cope with it, whether they agree with it or not. In the same fashion philosophers only recently have been able to minimize the reflections of Aristotle on the subject of logic.

Aristotle wrote exhaustively on the subjects of ethics and politics, producing the *Nicomachean Ethics* and the *Politics*. No contemporary college course treating of morality or ethics can fail to allot generous time to the *Ethics*, as no course in political theory can omit the *Politics*. Liberals might wish that Aristotle had sided with Democritus, Protagoras, and the Sophists against Plato, but he did not. Aristotle was as conservative as his teacher, holding to a belief that society should be hierarchically structured and governed in an authoritarian, though not despotic, fashion. Some men, states the *Ethics*, are born to be slaves; others by nature are destined to rule as masters. To Aristotle, women were to be completely subject to the will of men. Families were to have nothing to say in the control of education. Aristotle held Spartan views on education; it was a matter for state control because it was to form men as the state wished to have them. Hitler, Stalin, and all other modern totalitarians would have been pleased with these views.

THE HELLENIZATION OF ROME

Though Rome annexed the Hellenistic world between 197 and 146 B.C., Romans already had adopted Hellenistic education and general culture; Greece made captive her captors. There had been Greek colonies in Italy since the eighth century B.C., and when Rome absorbed those colonies (Magna Graecia) in the third century, she imported into Rome a great number of Greek teachers.

By this time, Greek schooling had arrived at its final form, a course of study divided into two parts, one which the Romans called the *quadrivium* (elementary level of schooling), composed of the study of arithmetic, geometry, astronomy, and music, the other, a secondary level consisting of the study of grammar, rhetoric, and logic, called the *trivium*. Physical education was not included by name but was taken for granted. The *quadrivium* and the *trivium* made up the seven liberal arts, as they came to be called, which made up the curriculum of European education for a thousand years to come.

Inspection of the liberal arts reveals some very interesting things. First, the Rhetorical Sophists seem to have had the greatest influence in its design. Their favorite subjects, grammar and rhetoric, occupy two-thirds of the *trivium*, in which Plato is not even represented. The logic of the *trivium*, the study prized by Aristotle, was not equivalent to the dialectic, the search after meanings, intended by Plato. It was a study of propositions epitomized by the syllogism, whose classic, Aristotelian form can be found in any textbook on formal logic. The sole Platonic study of the seven liberal arts was geometry, which came about as a result of the work of Euclid and other Hellenistic geometers, and not because Plato valued it for preparing the youthful mind.

In a word, the liberal arts which Greece and Rome gave in trust to western Europe exemplified the educational philosophy of Isocrates, endorsed by both Cicero and Quintilian, the two leading educational theorists of Rome. It should be noted that there is almost nothing in the writings of either Cicero or Quintilian which did not appear earlier in Isocrates' writings or the suggestions for education of the Elder Sophists. In *De oratore* (23), Cicero (106-43 B.C.) lent the prestige of his name to the idea that the teacher of oratory should be what Elder Sophists had termed a "polymath," a man at home in many subjects. (Today the equivalent phrase is "general education.") Nor did Cicero fail to agree with the Sophists that education should train men for the "art of politics" (statecraft), which Democritus had defined as the "capable administration of civic business." Cicero himself had taken advanced study in Greece, and was altogether under the sway of the rhetorical inheritance left by Isocrates.

BEYOND GREECE AND ROME

Through Cicero, and more notably from the *Institutes of Oratory* (24), written by Cicero's successor Quintilian (A.D. 35-100), the Middle Ages and the Renaissance received the thoughts of Greek educators. For a time the Christian church opposed the pagan humanism, but all the leading intellectuals of the Church were steeped in that pagan learning, and the very training in preaching was an attempt to copy the rhetoric polished by the Greeks and Romans.

Greek and Roman learning survived in Italy, despite the invasions of the Goths and other Germanic tribes. Hellenized Roman clergy had journeyed to England and humanism lived on there. It was from that island that the learned Christian monk, Alcuin, left for the barbaric court of Charlemagne in the eighth century A.D., accompanied by three humanist clerics, Clement, Joseph, and Dungal. At the court of Charlemagne, these three met their humanist peers from Italy, Paul the Deacon from Lombardy, Peter of Pisa, and Paulinus of Aquileia.

BIBLIOGRAPHY

1. BRAIDWOOD, ROBERT J., *The Near East and the Foundations for Civilization.* Eugene, Ore.: Oregon State System of Higher Education, 1952.

2. BREASTED, JAMES HENRY, *A History of Egypt.* New York: Charles Scribner's Sons, 1912.

3. CHIAPPE, ANDREW, *Five Comedies of Aristophanes.* New York: Columbia University Press, 1957.

4. CHIERA, EDWARD, *They Wrote on Clay*. Chicago: The University of Chicago Press, 1938.

5. CLARK, DONALD LEMEN, *Rhetoric in Graeco-Roman Education*. New York: Columbia University Press, 1957.

6. ERMAN, ADOLPH, *The Literature of the Ancient Egyptians*, tr. by A. M. Blackman. New York: E. P. Dutton & Co., Inc., 1927.

7. FREEMAN, KENNETH J., *Schools of Hellas*. London: Macmillan & Co., Ltd., 1908.

8. HAVELOCK, ERIC, *The Crucifixion of Intellectual Man*. Boston: Beacon Press., Inc., 1950.

9. ————, *The Liberal Temper in Greek Politics*. New Haven: Yale University Press, 1957.

10. HERSKOVITS, MELVILLE J., *Man and His Works*. New York: Alfred A. Knopf, Inc., 1947.

11. HUBBELL, HARRY MORTIMER, *The Influence of Isocrates on Cicero, Dionysius and Aristides*. New Haven: Yale University Press, 1914.

12. JAEGER, WERNER, *Paideia: The Ideals of Greek Culture*, 3 vols., tr. by Gilbert Highet. New York: Oxford University Press, 1945.

13. JASTROW, MORRIS, JR., *The Civilization of Babylonia and Assyria*. Philadelphia: J. B. Lippincott Co., 1915.

14. JONES, TOM B., *Ancient Civilization*. Chicago: Rand McNally & Co., 1960.

15. JOWETT, B., *The Dialogues of Plato*, 4 vols. New York: Charles Scribner's Sons, 1905.

16. LEAKEY, L. S. B., "Exploring 1,750,000 Years into Man's Past," *National Geographic*, CXX, No. 4 (1961), 564-589.

17. MCKEON, RICHARD, ed., *The Basic Works of Aristotle*. New York: Random House, Inc., 1941.

18. MARROU, H. I., *A History of Education in Antiquity*, tr. by George Lamb. New York: Sheed & Ward, 1956.

19. NORLIN, GEORGE, tr., *Isocrates*, Vol. II. London: William Heinemann, Ltd., 1928.

20. OLMSTEAD, A. T., *History of Assyria*. New York: Charles Scribner's Sons, 1923.

21. PARSONS, EDWARD A., *The Alexandrian Library*. Amsterdam: The Elsevier Press, 1952.

22. WATKINS, MARK HANNA, "The West African 'Bush School,'" *The American Journal of Sociology*, XLVIII, No. 6 (1943), 666-675.

23. WATSON, JOHN S., tr., *Cicero on Oratory and Orators*. London: George Bell & Sons, 1903.

24. ————, *Quintilian's Institutes of Oratory*, 2 vols. London: George Bell & Sons, 1903.

This chapter covers a period from A.D. 476 to
1400. Customarily, this span of almost a thousand
years has been divided into two portions, each
roughly five hundred years. The earlier half has
been named the Dark Ages, the latter half
the Middle Ages.

This division is an interesting one. Ostensibly,
to call the five hundred years that followed the
⊀ dislocation of the Western Roman Empire of
Rome (*c.* 476) the "Dark Ages" is to
point out that there existed in these centuries
no more than a cultural wasteland, that, in
effect, all things beautiful died with the
Western Roman Empire. It is as if to say
that the lamp of civilization had been snuffed
out, only to be feebly rekindled when the name
of Rome was revived, as it was in 962 when
Otto the Great of the German nation was
crowned Emperor of the Holy Roman
Empire. This was a splendid title for Otto's
empire; with the name *Roman* it was saved from
being a kingdom of barbarians, although, in
fact, Otto was no more tutored than his

20

EDUCATION
IN WESTERN
EUROPE
A. D. 476-1400

3

ancestor, Odacer, who had been the king of the Ostrogoths who captured Rome and added Italy to their kingdom.

Extending the idea that civilization, after the fall of Rome, awaited a renascence of Graeco-Roman culture, men have been accustomed to refer to the centuries after the crowning of Otto as the "Middle Ages." Again, the inference is that the five medieval centuries were a halfway house to the true revival of civilization that was to take place with the Renaissance. The name *Renaissance* means nothing more than revival. This under-estimation of the millennium separating the fall of Rome from the Renaissance is little less than astonishing. The Dark Ages might better be renamed a "period of transition" (12), and medieval times, the Middle Ages, recognized as centuries in which Europe developed a noteworthy and unique civilization.

A PERIOD OF TRANSITION

One of the reasons for the appellation "Dark Ages" for the period of transition has been the historical neglect of the commerce that actually criss-crossed Europe with trade routes, dotted it with markets and fairs, and kept its peoples in communication. Timber, metals, furs, and slaves were exported from the north of Europe; from the East came spices, silks, and the coveted Byzantine purple cloth. Economic historians have a favorite story to illustrate the fact that even the interior of western Europe was open to foreign traders. Gregory of Tours recorded that when King Guntram entered Orléans, he had been welcomed ". . . in Syrian, Latin, and Hebrew . . . in the sixth century these were the native tongues of the merchants of Orléans" (16:168).

Early in the period of transition there was a good deal of trade. Before the dawn of the Middle Ages, Postan (16) located traces of specialized communities of sheep-raisers, fishermen, salt harvesters, charcoal burners, and miners. All these specialists traded with one another in Europe, and conducted a bulk trade with the East (16:129). Some trade centers became large. The Frisians of what today is Holland spoke of the size of Dorstand on the old estuary of the Rhine by saying that it was a "city of forty cyrches" (16:176).

True enough, there was almost no Greek philosophy and literature available; Latin writing, except for a scant Church production, fell off in the sixth century. By 580, Latin was superseded by vernacular languages, even in Italy and Spain. But all vernacular was despised by the self-appointed custodians of culture. Latin was considered the sole vehicle of significant thought, the study of Latin grammar the principal study of schools. To the Latinophiles, the cultural darkness was almost unrelieved.

The disdain of the vernacular, the idea that no thought or feeling worthy of expression could be expressed in anything but Latin, persisted among educators throughout the period, keeping them out of touch with creative impulses that produced the beautiful Irish illustrations of the *Book of Kells* (718-732), and the heroic literature in the vernacular languages of the English, the Goths, the Norse sagas, the Anglo-Saxon *Beowulf*, and the French *Chanson de Roland*. Of course, not all vernacular literature was ignored by those schooled in Latin. The work of Caedmon, the Anglo-Saxon poet of the mid-seventh century, spread on the Continent because it was admired by Boniface (678-755), who founded the great school at Fulda, in Germany. But the Germans (Waldere, Finnsburgh, Maldon, and Hildebrand) were of almost no interest to learned grammarians.

Because of their preoccupation with Latin grammar, rhetoric, and logic—together with Christian philosophy and theology—the official educators of the period turned their backs on all folk art and science. The intellectual and artistic excellence of the period was ignored, leaving the age to be considered "dark." In this fashion the myth was created that the "light," the rebirth of civilization, lay in the centuries of the Renaissance. Renaissance intellectuals themselves began the custom of downgrading the centuries between the collapse of Imperial Rome and the fifteenth century. The highly creative fifteenth century writers, artists, scientists, and other thinkers felt themselves spiritually related to the great creators of the classic period of Greece and Rome. It was the German Nicholas of Cusa who, early in the fifteenth century, referred to the thousand-year period after the fall of Rome [1] as *media tempestas*, the "middle ages."

EXTENDING CHRISTIANITY AND RE-ESTABLISHING POLITICAL ORDER

Two lines of force run through the whole of the period of transition and the medieval times in western Europe. One was the effort of the Roman Catholic Church to Christianize Britain and Europe in the face of heresies and military threats from Arab, Moslems, and much later, the Turks. Intimately connected with this Christian endeavor was the warring between tribal groups who had probably been beaten into a semblance of political confederation by such a strong personality as Charlemagne. Never grasping the idea of empire (3:327), and looking on an empire as something to be divided up at the death of the king or emperor, the aristocracy of the tribes did exactly that shortly after the death of Charlemagne, and not without bloodshed.

The role of the Roman Catholic Church and the efforts at evolving an ongoing political state overlapped. When Charlemagne restored the Western Empire, the restoration was considered a plan of the Church, which

---

[1] It would be well to abandon the phrase "the fall of Rome." Evidence bears out the claim of Lopez (12) that the invading "barbari" wished to preserve the old Roman institutions, even the bad ones. After all, many of these invaders had lived within the Roman Empire for centuries. Continuity also was guaranteed by the Roman Catholic Church, whose official language had remained Latin.

". . . envisaged the emperor as a sort of universal magistrate responsible for prompting the faith and for protecting the Church" (3:326-327). In the administration of the empire, the clerks, judges, and other officials were supplied by the Church. The education of these scribes was a responsibility of the Church, and the art of writing, as well as Latin grammar and rhetoric (for teaching elegance of expression), became top studies.

From the sixth to the tenth century, the Church was the only agency of society that could conduct education; its achievement was not inconsiderable. As early as the eighth century, the bishops had laid upon them the duty to offer the rudiments of education to all who might ask for it (19:194). Though the duty was impossible to enforce, it was promulgated as official Church policy. In 826, the General Church Council of Pope Eugenius directed that "in bishops' sees and in other places where necessary, care and diligence should be exhibited in the appointment of masters and doctors to teach faithfully grammar and the liberal arts, because in them especially God's commands are made clear and explained" (4:115).

During the five centuries of transition from the collapse of the Roman world till the founding of the Holy Roman Empire under Otto in 962, the Church had as its most practical problem that of educating the clergy. Only an educated clergy could interpret God's commands written in the Scriptures, conduct the services of the Church, and help defend the faith against heresies. Clerics had to be able to read and write. One of the canons passed at the Council of Orléans in 533 stated that "a priest or deacon who is unlettered and does not know the baptismal service ought in no wise to be ordained" (20:11).

Defense against invasion of infidels (literally, those lacking the faith) and the spread of heretical notions spurred the Church to help the cause of education. The price, the unhappy price, of Christian zeal was that the Western Christian was hostile to anything that might be interpreted as the enemy of Christian doctrine. This led to provincialism, always the enemy of education and certainly an unfortunate characteristic of this period. Pope Gregory spoke of the hostility of St. Benedict, whose rules for monastic life governed the monasteries of the period, to Greek and Roman (pagan) literature. "St. Benedict," wrote Gregory, "chose to be knowingly ignorant and wisely unlearned" (4:103).

CHURCH SCHOLARS AND SCHOOLS
DURING THE PERIOD OF TRANSITION

Preserving classical learning. In the fourth and fifth centuries, the Romans opened grammar schools in Gaul. These schools remained when the Gauls moved against Rome (20:7). Nor was it surprising that municipal schools operating under the Romans in Italy and Spain continued to operate in the kingdom of the West Goths. Moreover, educated Romans became advisors to the Ostrogothic court in Rome, just as educated Greeks had been imported into Rome seven centuries earlier. One of these advisors was Cassiodorus (*c.* 490-585) who, though he could not convince the Gothic aristocracy to take up Roman learning, did serve the same end by arranging that grammar school teachers be paid by the Ostrogothic court (11:28). Cassiodorus built two monasteries on his ancestral estates, and in both had rooms for copying Roman manuscripts. The copying rooms, *scriptoria*, became a feature of almost all later monasteries. This fortunate arrangement became the prototype for later manuscript reproduction, as, for example, that of Servatus Lupus, abbot of Ferrières, France, between 842 and 862.

In Ireland, and later in England, Roman scholarship was especially fortunate. When St. Patrick came to Ireland in 432 to preach Christianity, he found tribes with highly tutored priests, the Druids, like the bards of Homer. By the seventh century, Ireland had become the European country best educated in Latin letters (4:107). There was at least one school of "Latin and Christian letters," as well as a school of Irish law and one of Irish literature (4:108).

Unhappily for Ireland, the Viking invasions interrupted this educational prosperity, and by the ninth century it was quite smothered.

England was reached by Christianity and Latin grammar a century after St. Patrick had begun his mission in Ireland, a lag that some Irish feel has never been overcome. Leach has it that the monk Augustine, Prior of Pope Gregory's own monastery of St. Andrew, came to England in 597 and was quickly able to convert the Kentish king, Ethelbert. Ethelbert had a Catholic wife that he had acquired from the Kingdom of the Franks. Within a year, during which Augustine visited Gaul and was made Bishop of Arles, he made his way back to England and founded simultaneously, in 598, England's first cathedral, Christ Church, and its first grammar school, attached to the cathedral.

Survival of the seven liberal arts. No phrase has held more magic for educators than "the seven liberal arts." Although Cicero had written and talked of the "liberal arts," it was Cassiodorus who made those arts magical by appending the number seven: "Wisdom builded her house; she has hewn out her seven pillars" (Prov. 9:1). In thus coupling the liberal arts with the Scriptures in *De artibus et disciplinus liberalium,* Cassiodorus typified the popularity of astrology and magic throughout the period.

The survival of the Hellenic course of study did not depend only on Cassiodorus. The Middle Ages had many who knew well the early fifth-century publication, *The Marriage of Philosophy and Mercury* by Marcianus Capella. Indeed, the extravagant imagery of Capella was irresistible to medieval rhetoricians. But it was neither Cassiodorus nor Capella who enjoyed the best reputation among educational theorists of the period of transition and the early Middle Ages. Boethius (481-525) carried off the honors both in general philosophy and in educational theory, for it was

Boethius who informed medieval schoolmen that the seven liberal arts might be divided into mathematical (scientific) and literary studies. This curricular division never died in Europe, where even today a secondary student can concentrate, to an extent, in the one or the other. The literary program has come to be classified as "humanistic," the mathematical and scientific course "realistic."

The monasteries that were built after the sixth century must not be overlooked. Not only did monks preserve Greek and Roman thought by copying manuscripts; some monks kept detailed notes on their studies (florilegia), wrote original compositions on saints' lives, wrote hymns, and so forth (19:185-186). Many monks had to learn the three R's, not only to keep the religious calendar of holy days, but to account for the farming operations of the monasteries, which held huge tracts of land and practiced skilled agriculture.

Outside the monasteries, there was a considerable amount of commerce that called for clerical skills, often supplied by clergy (clerks) (11:64).

The court schools. In the countryside, the only opportunity for education was in the court schools of kings and major aristocrats. There is no firm evidence of how numerous these court schools may have been, but that of Charlemagne was the best-known. Here, the presiding teacher was a learned monk, Alcuin, whom Charlemagne brought from York, England, to teach his children, himself, and young aristocrats at court. The fact that Charlemagne could come to kingship without being literate indicates that the Germanic aristocracy before the tenth century spent its time learning how to fight, hiring its literacy from the Church.

The art of letter-writing, especially the composition of official, ceremonious letters was of cardinal importance in the Middle Ages (2:208). Dictamen, writing letters for those who could not write, was a recognized profession and a habitual means of education. The model for the official correspondence of the Western world was the Papal Chancery. The chief center for the teaching of creative writing and dictamen was Bologna (2:208). And for the aid of clerical teachers of writing, there were collections of form letters and manuals (*ars distaminis*).

A boy or girl learned letters in a song school, before he or she was old enough to study Latin grammar. Even while in the Frankish court of Charlemagne, Alcuin kept up correspondence with his old school in York, advising its director to have three separate courses of study, one in handwriting, and separately, one in song and one in grammar. The song school took the place of the Roman *Ludus*, taught by the litterateur; the practical need for choirboys gave it its start. Gregory of Tours had evolved the plain song, the so-called Gregorian chant, around 590, and the song of choir

25

school, often attached to cathedrals, taught reading for obvious use. This school wins a place in a survey of the history of education because it was the ✳ first real opportunity for poor boys of this period who were of promising voice and intelligence to learn to read.

From song to grammar. When a boy could read he was ready for the study of Latin grammar. Although this grammar would be essential for any work in law, the chief impetus for grammatical study was in preparing a ✗ future churchman to interpret the highly symbolic language of the Bible. "It was . . . a limited and technical study," writes Atkins of the Latin grammar of the seventh and eighth centuries. "Its aim was purely utilitarian; and it became the means of adapting ancient culture to religious education, and of introducing men to the language and literature of the Church (1:41). Even when training in grammar was not specifically for understanding the Scriptures, the literature analyzed for grammatical structure always was ✗ Christian. The poetry and prose of classical pagan writers were ignored even by such authorties as Bede (673-735), who inaugurated the study of Latin grammar in England, and, incidentally, led to the founding of the school at York from which Alcuin left for the court of Charlemagne. Other schools opened in the tenth century, in Great Britain and on the Continent, some in connection with cathedrals (as the school at Chartres, where the director of the school bore the old Latin title for a secondary school teacher, *grammaticus*).

The grammar books of Bede and Alcuin were simple indeed, for their students had most modest literary backgrounds. For all teachers of grammar there were simple texts written by Bede, Alcuin, Boniface, and others such as Paulus, Diaconus, Loup, Remi, Gerbert (also at Chartres Cathedral, but in the eleventh century), Abbo, and Aelfric (2:130).

From grammar to rhetoric. Even as rhetoric was the chief liberal study of Athens and Rome, gradually taking the foremost place in the *trivium*, in Alcuin's hands it was training in political rule or governance. It was the ✗ art of persuasion of one's subjects, to be employed by kings as well as popes. One of the masterpieces of medieval *political* rhetoric was delivered at Claremont in 1095, when Pope Urban "preached a crusade," persuading the kings and princes of Europe to recover the Holy Land. Urban practiced what he had read in the fourth book of *De doctrina Christiana*, where St. ✗ Augustine reminded his readers that rhetoric was a means of moving men to truth, of preaching the word of God. Alcuin simply changed the role of the orator from Christian preacher to lay ruler. His little book on rhetoric, written for his royal pupils Charlemagne and his son, was written in dialogue form, drawing freely on Cicero's *De inventione*. The cases cited are taken from Cicero, and the rhetoric really was part of the Ciceronian study of law. Centuries later at Bologna, Italy, this "judicial" branch of rhetoric was to give rise to the first European university study of law.

For teaching the art of preaching, medieval teachers also had manuals and models. The thesaurus of Jacques de Vitry (died in 1240) was systematically practical, a collection not primarily *of* sermons, but *for* sermons. Models, outlines, suggestions, intended for adaptation in the vernacular were arranged according to the Church calendar (2:234-235).

Legal rhetoric made room for literary rhetoric, the medieval sire of all contemporary literary study. The creator of that early literary rhetoric was a student of Alcuin's, Rabanus Maurus (776-856). Atkins, partisan to grammatical and rhetorical study only when associated with literature (rather than with law or a scientific study of language structure), was delighted to find Rabanus Maurus "rescue" rhetoric from Alcuin's preoccupation with training Charlemagne as a ruler (1:61-62).

From rhetoric to dialectic. The practical application of rhetoric to civil affairs and to preaching did little to hold the attention of the philosophers of the Middle Ages. For them, rhetoric was to serve as an aid to analysis of arguments in law or in theology. Serving these ends, rhetoric no longer could be a study for the young. The time had come for the full revival of Aristotelian logic and the emergence of the university. The period of transition had merged into the Middle Ages.

2. A GREAT MOVE FORWARD: Education During the Middle Ages, 962-1200

DEVELOPMENTS IN THE ECONOMY

The most interesting development in rural Europe during the Middle Ages was feudalism. Although the legends of feudal King Arthur and his Knights of the Round Table were still evolving during the latter half of the Middle Ages, at the same time thriving, new towns—some quite large— gave evidence of interesting urban life, making improvements in the European economy indispensable. Indeed, the volume of trade increased many times over what it had been during the period of transition (16:159). The population of western Europe also grew dramatically (3:349), and most important for education, began to center in towns and cities. By the twelfth century, urban centers such as Venice and Genoa in Italy "had surpassed in wealth the greatest business centres of the classic world" (12:289).

In agriculture, the sophistication of the Romans, who knew well the utility of growing a leguminous crop alternately with grain, was almost lost in the invasions of the fifth century. With the first years of the Middle Ages, improvements began. It first was necessary to break the barbarians to the plow, to make them farmers rather than raiders. This was done by the ninth century, and during the next four hundred years Europeans learned to drain large areas of land and to farm with increasing technological skill. Not only did over-all agricultural production increase, but different regions were able to specialize in crops (6:159).

Medieval knowledge expanded with insistent vigor. Whether it is in terms of care of the soil or of animals—breeding, harnessing, and shoeing—the eleventh and twelfth centuries cannot be considered primitive. Nor were they primitive in the mechanization of industry; watermills and windmills became the most conspicuous bits of scenery in medieval Europe, and where they could be seen the work of men was being mechanized.

A depression during the fourteenth and fifteenth centuries affected towns and the countryside as well. There were losses in population; some industries were hard hit while other enterprises progressed. North German trade, dominated by the great Hanseatic League, managed to prosper throughout the fourteenth century, greatly aided by the development of the *kogge*, a boat with wide, rounded sides, used for importing raw materials.

Urban population had swelled until the depression. Bruges, then part of France, had become a leading western port, trading regularly with Genoa in Italy. In 1352, Barker reports the population of Bruges to have stood at approximately 30,000 (3:422); for the late Middle Ages, this was a sizable city. The largest of medieval cities was Paris, which at the same time had some 200,000 inhabitants.

Population began to increase in the sixteenth century. In many cities—principally in Italy—banking had become an important business, one whose very essence was arithmetic. The development in Italy of bills of exchange and double-entry bookkeeping made possible the control of commercial activities on a vast scale. A bank in Italy could disburse monies in Bruges by simultaneously using its Italian assets and those of its client in Bruges. It was necessary only that banks in both countries make the necessary additions and subtractions in the accounts. To supply the needed bookkeepers and the necessary arithmetic and mathematical knowledge, the commercial interests put constant pressure on education, a pressure which the Church did not satisfy.

In arithmetic, the press during the Middle Ages was for the development of a rapid system of calculation, manipulation of Roman numerals being too difficult for keeping accounts (19:187-188). No significant progress was made, however, although the abacus was introduced into Europe, the Arabic number system was not to become generally known till late in the medieval period.

There is little question that medieval competence in geometry was far behind what had been achieved in Hellenistic times. This could be said of scientific knowledge generally, but *not* of applied science, the "mechanical arts," or as they were commonly called, the "fabrile arts." Indeed, applied science and technology stimulated a study of theoretical or basic science (6:147), not the reverse, *which became the case only after the seventeenth century*. For example, the widespread use of the abacus prompted the medieval study of a theory of numbers or theoretical arithmetic. Mathematical researches were given a boost, and by the thirteenth century it was common to think in terms of abstract, standardized units. The art and science of measuring could now move ahead of where it had been in ancient Egypt and Babylonia. By the end of the thirteenth century, the mechanical clock was invented, translating units of time into units of space on a dial. Space itself was plotted into units, maps of the fourteenth century showing the world divided into squares according to latitude and longitude (6:150).

The increasing sophistication both in musical techniques and theory is not to be overlooked in reviewing the medieval developments of the *quadrivium* (6:151-155). By the opening of the tenth century, there were written descriptions of harmony, singing a tune at two different pitches. The next two centuries witnessed a great elaboration in diaphony. The course of development is evident in the evolution of the Gregorian plain chant of the seventh century into the counterpoint of the thirteenth century, and the elaborate polyphony of the masses in the fourteenth and fifteenth centuries.

OTHER EVIDENCE OF SCIENTIFIC SOPHISTICATION

In the great Gothic cathedrals, medieval mechanical art and science is strikingly manifest. The vaulted roofs of these amazing buildings were made possible during the twelfth century by the understanding of stress—an understanding that involved geometry as well as mechanics.

Shipping that was indispensable to commerce could be adventurous, since mariners had more accurate maps to tell them of their locations. Metal working and glassmaking—both requiring more than a smattering of industrial chemistry made possible the brass of cannons, the painter of houseware, and the stained glass in the windows of cathedrals.

FEUDALISM AND EDUCATION

Although there certainly was an upper class (patriciate) in medieval towns, membership in it was dependent only on wealth. The dependence of social position or status on money was foreign to the concept of *aristocracy* (which continues to mean more than simply having wealth). To be an aristocrat meant to be titled—to hold a title to land that could be inherited. In the tenth century, the aristocrats were kings and their warrior knights, the most important of these warrior nobles holding large grants of land from the king. The relation of king to knight and knight to king, and of both to serfs who worked the lands, was one of *dependence*. This quality of dependence was quite similar to that which characterizes a patriarchal family: the king was father, the knights dependent uncles, and the peasants were children to be cared for while obedient and chastised when willful.

By 1100, the class structure in rural Europe had solidified. Knights became *hereditary* aristocrats, a nobility which succeeded in remaining the upper class for many centuries. Even when the burghers of the town became merchant princes they acquired titles either by direct gifts of the kings or by marrying their daughters to title-bearing but poorly landed aristocracy. For education, the result of freezing the rural class structure meant that very few young people from the lower classes could anticipate rising in life because of their merits. The only ladder was the monastery and service in the Church. It is highly questionable whether this blocking of opportunity for lower-class youth ever truly changed in rural Europe. Only by leaving the land for the city was there an open door.

In sum, any discussion of education in rural Europe, where ninety-five per cent of the population lived, focuses on the education of the feudal aristocracy, on the education of lords and vassals.

Education of knight and lady. The education of the rural aristocracy was an adaptation of the liberal arts. Boys had to learn to ride horseback and to fight mounted and in dismount. There was physical exercise that would have been perfectly acceptable to any Spartan of the sixth and fifth centuries B.C.

While most of the time for the education of boys was devoted to training for war, the philosophy of feudal education was built on the *ideal of brotherhood.* For the aristocracy, brotherhood literally meant the helpfulness that brothers in a fraternity show each other. Only the Church tried to extend this provincial or limited fraternalism to include the weak and the needy of Christendom. Since there is too little evidence to conclude that the Church indulged the teaching of dancing and music in an effort to gentle the warrior-knights, it may be said that these gentle arts probably were taught in order to make more livable the otherwise dismal court life of the feudal castles and manors.

A squire of twenty (as in Chaucer's prologue to the *Canterbury Tales*) might have served as a page or valet from six or seven till fourteen. During these years, in which the ladies of the court would look after him, he was expected to learn polite manners (*noblesse oblige*, literally, these manners obligatory for the noble- or gentleman), singing, reading, writing, and arithmetic. Without any regard for what Plato or any other Hellene said about the gentling effect of music, the feudal court encouraged traveling minstrels to compose, as well as perform, verse set to music. Undoubtedly this was the manner in which vernacular literature and music, apart from the plain song or chant of the Church, were introduced to feudal society. That folk art and music lived on in Europe during the Middle Ages was due to the demand of the feudal court for entertainment.

The twelfth and the thirteenth centuries comprised the great age of the troubadours and trouveres in courts of France, and of the minnesingers in those of Germany. To help the ladies of the court instruct both boys and girls in courtly manners there were a number of "courtesy books." Around 1266, Vincent of Beauvais published his *Of the Instruction of Girls of Noble Lineage*. Apparently the English were especially keen on the teaching of *courtesy*, the manner of the court, for they had available such titles as *The Babee's Book, Stand Boy at the Table, Of Manners to Bring One to Honor and Welfare*, and *Learne or be Lewde*.

For slightly older children, specially boys, there was a "literature of example," functioning as did the Homeric epics. Of great repute in medieval feudal circles were the *Song of Roland* in France, and in England, Geoffrey of Monmouth's *The History of British Kings*.

When a boy left the care of the ladies and began to learn his chief task, that of fighting on horseback, his male tutors—usually his father or uncles, as in any tribe—might use such an elaborate textbook as that by Christie of Pisa (*c.* 1364-1429), *The Fayt of Arms and of Chyvalry*. This, or another, might be read during the five years of squirehood preceding knighthood, which took place at age twenty-one.

Reception into the brotherhood of knights was the crowning ceremony of feudalism. In most respects it was like a *rite de passage* of a preliterate group. As with most preliterate tribes, the ceremony was religious and involved purification. The sword that marked the knight came to him from an altar, and held hilt upright, it made the sign of the cross. The young knight had both secular and sacred allegiances, secular and sacred wisdom to sustain and perpetuate.

EDUCATION IN TOWN, AND BY THE LAITY

A student of the history of education cannot but be impressed with the few opportunities for education children of the poor, of the lowest social classes, have had. In the towns of the Middle Ages, there was at least opportunity for very practical training, furnished by the medieval guilds, which became the first successful, organized forms of vocational education. Moreover, the guilds were not bound by any conventions appropriate to the class background of apprentices. Sons of artisan or merchant members of the guild were the most likely candidates for apprenticeship, but any likely lad could be apprenticed without any concern about his social standing. This lack of social class-consciousness existed just as long as medieval urban society retained a fluid quality.

Although there was stratification in medieval urban society, it was fluid; there was no tradition comparable to the feudal tradition of knighthood. Competition was much more the rule in a merchant community than in the brotherhood of a knightly class. Merchants had no time for versifying, dancing, jousting in tournament, or cultivating physical grace and strength.

Aggressive and imaginative enterprise became the bourgeois virtue, a virtue that the rural aristocracy grew to despise, and of which the very wealthy merchants of later centuries learned to be so ashamed that they sent their children to schools where *feudal noblesse* could be taught.

Education in the guilds. Perhaps the most effective education in the Middle Ages was offered by the craft guilds. Certainly it had the highest standards, offering the only education with periodic, rigorous examinations —examinations that demanded top performance. As we shall see, the guild perfected a model for training that was adopted by the first universities. This unquestioned excellence has made the lack of attention to guild training by educational historians all the more puzzling. Perhaps this neglect is due to the fact that the guild did not offer its apprentices and journeymen (the urban equivalent of valet and squire) a general education, instruction in the liberal arts beyond reading, writing, and arithmetic. The guilds were strictly vocational in objective, aiming at specialization, which has always been denied a high status in the history of education.

Lasting from five to eleven years, and starting with boys who were not to be younger than seven, guild education prospered throughout the late Middle Ages and into the early Renaissance. Aside from the fact that a guild could fix prices and conditions of work, the attractiveness of the guild arrangement to university students and to teachers was the protection the power of the group afforded its members (15:63). The importance of guild organizations and associations of merchants as well, to universities was very great, as can be seen by terminology. For example, the term *university* originates with the *universitas* of towns, associations of leading families for the exercise of political power (15:49). The term *college* has been used at Oxford since the thirteenth century to denote places where students could find board, room, and instruction. The literal Latin derivation of college is *colegio*, "to read together." Originally, Romans in the second century A.D. used the term *collegia* for groups of craftsmen or merchants, the idea of association to promote shared interests and welfare having been borrowed by them from an earlier Greek model (22:59). The mutuality of interests and welfare, characteristic of colleges and universities in all later times, is modeled after that earlier fraternalism of artisan and merchant.

The schools of the town. The municipal schools of today have inherited a colorful past, for there is no more interesting episode in the history of education than that of the creation of schools under the control of lay authorities in medieval towns and cities. It is an episode concerned with struggle for power, and is in many other educational chronicles known only in a distorted version as a play for power between Church and laity.

In every town of the Middle Ages, there was likely to be a *scholasticus* with one or more teachers under his supervision. The scholasticus, a cleric under the jurisdiction of the bishop, was a licensed teacher, appointed and paid by the bishop. He might be the only person in the town who could write well. His services were in greater demand as business and commerce grew, and by the fourteenth century a single scholasticus was unable singly to cope with the needs of a town. This would have been enough to create pressure for more training in writing. Adding force to the demand for the scholasticus was the realization of many parents that writing, grammar, and reading were the best ways of entering a clerk's or a clerical life. As in ancient Mesopotamia and Egypt, becoming a scribe was perceived as an obvious means of improving one's economic and social position.

The advantages of having a number of boys who were able to write and read certainly were not lost on the merchant-burghers of the cities. The more literate boys there were, the easier it would be to find an able clerk, and the more independent would the merchant be from the scholasticus. Before the end of the thirteenth century, all the principal towns of the Netherlands had controlled municipal schools.

Though the struggle of the scholasticus to hold onto his well-paying scribal work was difficult (8:823), more important was the fact that the Church was now willing to withdraw from such worldly responsibilities as supplying notaries, lawyers, and judges. Indeed, the experience of the Church during the fourteenth century, when it had been all too worldly, had led to a renewed dedication to the things that are God's rather than Caesar's.

It is tempting to think of the municipal reading and writing schools or the Latin grammar schools, supported and controlled by the towns, as evidences of a first split between Church and state over control of education, but there is too little evidence to support this idea. More accurately, the towns were anxious to be as independent as possible of all outside forces, not only that of the Church, and there was the real need of parents and others for more training than was supplied by the Church. A third factor prompting town schools was the need for boys able to use the vernacular language. A merchant trading all over Europe and outside Europe would find Latin—as well as Greek and Arabic—useful, but within his own town, a local merchant needed a clerk who knew German or whatever the language was of the area in which he traded. Church schools taught Latin, and had the Church strained to provide instruction in the vernacular languages and arithmetic it might have kept its monopoly in licensing teachers for some little time, even if not in all programs for instruction of children. But the Church was uninterested in vernacular language, and even in the spread of knowledge of arithmetic. Thus when it insisted on being able to license all teachers, permission to operate vernacular schools was given towns by the reigning prince in the area in which the town was located. As a concession to the Church, the municipal schools of Brussels, authorized around 1320, were permitted to teach *only* in the vernacular; instruction in Latin, presumably a superior form of education, was reserved to the Church. This was but a temporary mollification of the Church, however; the thin end of

33

the wedge had been inserted. Moreover, when the local bishops, at the behest of the scholasticus, appealed to the pope, the latter was apt to side with the town (8:823-824).

The Renaissance was a time of genuine excitement about learning. Although this intellectual zest almost always is interpreted in terms of renewed interest in classical literature and philosophy, it is likely that the enthusiasm was a good deal more general. Perhaps the rise of the middle class can account for the fact that apathy toward education, at least in towns, was ended in the Renaissance. This is quite likely simply because the interest in education manifested in towns was middle class or bourgeois.

> Local interest in education was exceedingly great. Every prosperous community took pride in founding schools. They also founded bursaries (scholarships) for a multitude of students who otherwise would have remained ignorant. The citizens gave alms most indulgently to poor students and frequently took them into their homes. The Brethren of the Common Life not only provided many students with quarters in their "houses," but had no difficulty in persuading citizens to take in from one to eight pupils without compensation. Moreover, people of wealth provided for the endowment of scholarships, colleges, and the employment of teachers in their wills.
>
> So great was the demand for the arts of writing and reading that no town was without a school under the control of and in some cases, largely if not wholly, supported by the civil authorities. Practically all the people of the middle class learned to read and write (8:824).

3. COLLEGIATE SCHOOL AND UNIVERSITY IN THE THIRTEENTH CENTURY

The creation of universities is the educational climax of the Middle Ages. Three conditions made them possible, not the least of which was the existence of large towns and cities. Men interested in philosophy, theology, law, or medicine found the medieval city a good place in which to congregate. In a medieval city there was a great deal of coming and going and a great number of foreigners, many of them from the East and acquainted with the philosophy and science of Plato, Aristotle, and their Hellenistic successors. As in ancient Athens, the seaports and fair-towns of Europe were cosmopolitan—a condition always attractive to the inquiring, the curious of mind.

Most important of all, the Church had had a measure of success in carrying out the spirit of the General Church Council of 862, commanding the bishops to make education available to all who would learn. Associated with the cathedrals of the bishops were schools, first song schools and choir schools (*schola cantorum*), that could be described as elementary. The cathedral schools then added grammar, a secondary school offering during the eleventh century. Although the secondary cathedral schools have been completely overshadowed by the universities, the universities, in most instances, developed from them.

There are exceptions to this genetic rule, as in the instance of the Italian and Spanish schools of law and medicine. Unlike the University of Paris, which did have its roots in the schools associated with the Cathedral of Notre Dame, higher education in Italy and in Spain could emerge independently of the cathedral schools. Why? Because in both places the old Roman *municipal* secondary grammar schools had survived and made cathedral schools much less important. Moreover, Spanish cities like Toledo and Salamanca did not have to await the middle of the twelfth century to rejuvenate the advanced study of philosophy and logic. The Arab Moslems, with their translations and commentaries on Aristotle and all the later Greek philosophers and scientists, had kept Spanish intellectual life far in advance of that in northern Europe. In Italy, Roman law had been kept alive in the studies of the papacy. This was not secular law but canon or Church law, a mixture of law and theology; even so, it was no great effort for the city of Bologna to provide advanced study of law for secular, political administration as well as for the governance of the Roman Catholic Church.

For the most part, however, whether it was for the study of law, requiring firm grounding in grammar, rhetoric, and logic, or of medicine, philosophy, or theology, university training rested on a foundation of secondary school studies, even as it does today.

35

THE "WANDERING SCHOLAR" AND MEDIEVAL SOPHIST

By the eleventh century there was general, even popular, interest in intellectual questions. "The teaching of the Church was beginning to stir a lively response at all levels of society" (19:195). And there was quite a large, "floating" population of would-be scholars who were willing to go anywhere in their search for learning. Those interested in the law, rhetoric, or medicine might have found their way to Italy. But for the study of logic and grammar, which for the medieval scholar meant the meanings and derivations of words as well as the rhetorical rules of eloquence, France had more to offer. Exactly as the intellectual interests of Hellas in the fifth century B.C. had given rise to the Sophists, the intellectual interests of the early Middle Ages created the new Sophists, the free-lance teachers, some of whom, like some of their Hellenic predecessors, found teaching quite lucrative (19:196). Those among the medieval Sophists who had not the ability to make their living as freelancers found that they could teach and study in the cathedrals.

There were great cathedral schools in the eleventh and twelfth centuries.

On the Continent, one of the first, the school of greatest repute for at least a century, was the collegiate school of Chartres. Fulbert, later Bishop of Chartres, was chancellor. Adelman, Fulbert's student, praised his teacher as "the venerable Socrates of the Academy of Chartres."

Fulbert was but one of the bishop-chancellors whose cathedral schools in the eleventh and early twelfth centuries gave rise to the universities of the twelfth and thirteenth centuries. In France during the ninth, tenth, and eleventh centuries there were the schools of Rheims, Tours, Angers, and Lyons. But in Fulbert, and in the circle of students and scholars drawn to his cathedral, is visible the intellectual interests complementing Christian subjects that had to find expression before there could be intellectual life sufficient to support the universities.

What is important about the cathedral collegiate schools in the history of education is the fact that they were places where men learned, if not to master classical learning, at least to be knowledgeable about what had been achieved in Greece and Rome. The metaphysical and scientific works of Aristotle had yet to impress themselves on the Western mind, but when they came in the middle of the twelfth century, there were scholars who could read them with excitement, rather than with a sense of shock, thinking them at once alien and threatening. By the end of the twelfth century, the past no longer was a stranger to the present.

36

FROM SCHOLASTICUS TO CHANCELLOR

Changes in administrative structure, increases in the numbers of administrative officers and titles, always have been a sure sign of empires being built. So it was with the cathedral school of the twelfth century, where that old worthy of Roman days, the scholasticus, was still to be found. In medieval Rome the scholasticus, like his ancient predecessor, the grammaticus, taught grammar; in later centuries this meant teaching parts of speech and what was felt to be proper usage. But the scholasticus who had been the lowly, poorly paid Roman schoolteacher had risen to chancellor of a cathedral by the twelfth century, from which post it was but a step to being a chief officer of any university associated with a cathedral of a bishop's see. This was an impressive rise in status for one who had been a teacher of grammar in a cathedral school. The past had been improved upon by transferring the duty of teaching grammar to a member of the secular clergy who became the "grammar-school master." The chancellor became a master of theology, the most highly esteemed university subject.

THE MEDIEVAL UNIVERSITY

Although European universities grew according to no one plan, their history has enough in common to permit referring to it as *a* history of the university.

Paris in the twelfth century serves as illustration. Those who came to Paris to study with a master whose reputation had become known throughout Europe came from many countries. The cosmopolitan origins of the *studium* really were all that distinguished them from the local students in the grammar schools. Since they were from many nations, they were without protection in Paris. To gain the safety which comes from banding together, they formed associations, collegia, whose purposes we have identified as much like those of the guilds of the artisans.

The association between the university and business, commerce, and manufacture was an ancient one, as has been noted, long antedating the twelfth and thirteenth centuries. Walbank found collegia, as early as the second century A.D., in Rome, which had imported them from Hellenistic Greece, where it had been customary for free tradesmen, craftsmen, and professional workers to organize themselves in guilds whose functions included making regular contributions to pay for the funeral expenses of members (22:59).

By the middle of the thirteenth century, Paris had 101 such guilds (15:65); the students and masters of the city could see for themselves what a useful device the guild was in a town where local tradesmen and keepers of rooming houses were only too willing to exploit a student, especially a foreigner.

For too long the aggressiveness of the guilds has been overshadowed by their primary aim of affording members protection from exploitation. The students and masters of Paris and other towns would have observed the guilds in such aggressive maneuvers as that against the large-scale importers and exporters who wished to limit local manufacture and sale (15:65). Then, too, the guilds were pushing for greater political power.

Though the groups formed by students were modeled after the guild, they took the names "universities." The name, as we have seen, was borrowed from the *universitas*, associations in which the most politically powerful families of towns often were joined (15:49). While the term *college* implied the desire to give mutual aid and comfort, it was significant that the term *university* had no such dependent connotation; the universities intended to be independent, and if possible, powerful. Independent they did become, but powerful they did not.

Masters came to Paris before the students, who followed, attracted by their scholarly reputation. This priority in time meant that there were societies or universities of masters before the students organized their own. Though the student universities had fraternal protection in common with the guilds, the universities of the masters were more professionally guild-like. For one thing, the masters' universities evolved rules of training; before one could become a master, it was necessary for him to serve five to seven years as an apprentice or disciple of a recognized master. One of the early struggles of the university had been fought to win the right of the masters to supervise the apprenticeship of their fellows. That today an American faculty member will have his academic credentials judged by his colleagues, rather than by the administrative officers of the college, is a result of the right established in Paris in the thirteenth century.

Of course, not all the masters belonged to one university. There were the arts masters, called a "faculty" from the Latin *facultas*, meaning "power," and there were masters of theology, law, and medicine. As they had found strength in being joined in their individual faculties, the masters of the several faculties would band together into a single "corporation," as like the great merchant and banking corporations. By the end of the thirteenth century, the universities of masters all were joined in corporations, led by the Faculty of Arts. From this faculty a master would be elected to serve a term as rector of the corporation.

The curriculum of the medieval university. As one might imagine from the guild form of association, the course of study for a student during the twelfth century was rather like the study of a young man who wished to become a master craftsman. A student studied with, or was apprenticed to, a master in law, theology, or philosophy, and after about five years had to stand an examination, after which he could be presented to a chancellor or other Church official for licensing. The induction of a student into the ranks of the masters came to be a matter of considerable ceremony, but the principle of apprenticeship and examination by the masters of the academic guild was basic.

In the thirteenth century, Paris had a definite course of study for a student who wished to study for "the degree in arts"—the baccalaureate. A drastically modified version of the seven liberal arts was actually what he studied. Aristotle's works occupied a fair share of the readings and lectures.

By the fourteenth century there was a clear distinction between levels of degree, the lowest being the baccalaureate, followed by the "license" and, last, the master's degree. Today, in the United States, the "license" has become the master's degree and the master's degree has become the doctor's degree. *Doctor* was a medieval term, applied to such men as Thomas Aquinas, who came to be hailed as the "Angelic Doctor." Perhaps the degree of doctorate was evolved to distinguish an academic master from the master of a craft guild. If so, it was but recognition of the fact that the academic masters enjoyed a social status very much higher than that of craftsmen, however skilled. By the fourteenth century, academic prestige was great; kings and popes, princes and leading burghers competed for distinguished masters and academic corporations. In order to entice them, these officials would grant them the privilege of being tried in ecclesiastical courts, which gave immunity from the courts of the town. In this and in other ways, the early universities were protected and encouraged.

The manner of teaching in the medieval university. The intellectual craze of the time was for the preparation of summas, compendiums, and summaries of various fields of knowledge developed in the past. Peter Lombard prepared the most popular summa to be used as a text in theology in medieval universities. The title of his book, *Four Books of Sentences*, did not carry the word *summa*, but a summa it was all the same. Almost as notable and enduring was the legal summa of canon law prepared by Gratian about 1140 under the lyrical title, *Concordance of Discordant Canons*. There were many others—all popular textbooks—but none was more important than the *Summa theologica* of St. Thomas Aquinas.

It was not possible for students to have summas of their own, although there were dealers who lent them for a price. A master would have the summa or text for his course, reading from it and commenting on it after a passage had been read. The students attempted to copy what was read, hooting the professor if he read too fast.

As one would guess, it became standard procedure for a master to read, comment, and then invite questions. But medieval students who had made great sacrifices for their learning were genuinely caught up in the desire to know; questions simply were not enough, and "disputations" were added. Perhaps Peter Abelard (1079-1142) can be credited with introducing the disputation, a genuine debate over theological and philosophical points, although his method was an adaptation of the old Platonic dialectic and the analyses that had been perfected by the Greek and Roman rhetoricians. In its final medieval form, the disputation had as its object the reconciling or clarifying of seemingly contradictory statements. The need for reconciliation was obvious, and Abelard may have found his model in the work of such men as Ivo of Chartres, who in the tenth century had undertaken to reconcile contradictory statements appearing in pronouncements of Church Councils and in papal decrees. A reconciliation sought to arrive at reasoned decisions, not simply authoritative statements. It was a process that appealed to legal and philosophic minds and was the most effective antidote for the authoritarianism that came naturally to those more interested in power than truth or justice.

The wielder of power in the medieval university. Originally, the chancellor of a cathedral was head of the cathedral school, and as such was the representative of the bishop and the chief authority in educational administration for the city and the university, if the city had one. Every person who desired to teach, at the university or elsewhere, had to receive a license from the chancellor, and in some instances from the bishop sitting with the chancellor. Not only did the chancellor claim the right to give, withhold, or take away the license, but he insisted that masters and students be completely under his jurisdiction in matters of government and discipline. The masters objected; they recognized the chancellor's right to confer the license, but asserted that it was for them as a guild to fix the conditions of mastership, and they refused to allow any to enter their ranks who had not conformed to their regulations. To the officials of the Church in Paris this demand for autonomy constituted rebellion against authority. In the first decade of the thirteenth century, the chancellor began the contest in earnest by requiring all masters to swear obedience to himself. The masters met this move by appealing to Pope Innocent III, who decided in their favor. In the Bull of 1212, the chancellor was forbidden to exact an oath of obedience from the masters and was required to confer the license gratuitously on all candidates put forward by them. Only in the Faculty of Arts was the chancellor given partial control. In spite of the papal judgment, the local ecclesiastics continued their efforts to reduce masters and students to subjection, and actually excommunicated the whole university body when they drew up statutes for their own government. Again and again appeal was made to Rome, and the decisions, as before, were mainly in favor of the university. The chancellor's prison was abolished and the excommunication of the university forbidden without the express sanction of the pope (4:143).

At the close of the Middle Ages, the masters of the University of Paris were supreme, and the chancellor's privileges were limited to the ceremonial right of conferring license. The same events left the philosophers in the Faculty of Arts academically free. Between 1210 and 1277, the university won an independence all universities have fought to preserve ever since.

One of the most exciting and far-reaching series of events turned the University of Paris upside-down during much of the thirteenth century and established an age-long precedent of academic freedom. Academic freedom, of course, simply means that the academic staff of a college or university shall have the right to teach or publish what they deem proper. This right rests on the responsibility of the scholar, a responsibility to pursue truth with no holds barred. The trial and condemnation of Socrates in Athens had involved academic freedom, but at that time the Sophists were not banded together into an academic fraternity. Socrates, therefore, could not and did not plead academic freedom, but only the right of a man to follow the dictates of his own conscience. Such a plea always is less powerful in society than the plea of academic freedom, for within the academic community each scholar is under the scrutiny of his colleagues. Standards of scholarship, albeit unwritten, are staunchly held. Many people know this and therefore are willing to protect academic freedom. But even the most knowledgeable, within the academic life and without, have forgotten their indebtedness to the Faculty of Arts of the University of Paris, and to Popes Innocent III, Gregory IX, and Urban IV, all of whom sided with the masters of art against the bishops of Paris and the less than tolerant masters of theology.

Although the dramatic action of this series of events centers in the thirteenth century, the story can be traced back to the eighth century, when the Caliph of Bagdad, who had a great respect for Hellenistic learning, ordered the translation of Aristotle's works into Arabic. The manuscripts that the Caliph's translators used were not written in Greek but in Syriac; the original Greek already had been interpreted, and was to be reinterpreted in being rendered from Syriac into Arabic.

Arab scholars became enormously interested in Aristotle, and at least two Arabs, Avicenna (A.D. 980-1037) and Averroes (1126-1198), wrote remarkable commentaries on his philosophy. Arab philosophical scholarship flourished not only in Bagdad but in the westernmost reaches of the Arab world, in Spain. There the Arab translations of Aristotle, together with the commentaries of Averroes, attracted the scholarly notice of a truly formidable thinker, the Jewish philosopher Maimonides (1135-1204). In Arab and Jewish hands, the non-Christian elements of Aristotle's thought were anything but hidden. The idea of eternal matter, of the impossibility of individual immortality—both ideas found in Aristotle—were freely noted. Little wonder that the Council of Sens, Paris, 1210, forbade lecturing on Aristotle. The ban seemed not too successful, however, and in 1215 the commentaries of Aristotle again were banned. In defense of the Council of Sens, the bishops of Paris, and the masters of theology, it must be admitted that Aristotle's thought had gone through too many translations. Original meanings in crucial passages had been lost. The Church had become a bit touchy throughout the thirteenth century because there had been a spread of alarming heresies, such as the Albigensian heresy in southern France.

What finally saved the day for the Aristotelians among the masters of arts were the good translations of Aristotle by William of Moerbke, later Archbishop of Corinth, who knew Greek and completed a translation of Aristotle at the request of St. Thomas Aquinas (c. 1225-1274) in 1267. The commentaries of Albertus Magnus (1193-1280) and St. Thomas Aquinas won acceptance for Aristotle. In 1265, Pope Urban IV officially approved Aristotelian philosophy, which henceforth became so well-accepted that it stifled creative thinking in philosophy and prepared the way for the sixteenth century revolt against scholasticism. The fighting spirit of the anti-Aristotelian members of the University of Paris Faculty of Theology, joined again by Tempier, Bishop of Paris, was displayed for the last time between 1270 and 1277; Aristotelian teaching again was banned in Paris, but the ban was short-lived. Even the masters of theology, led by Godfrey of Fontaines, who taught theology at Paris from 1286-1300, came to condemn the ban on Aristotelian teaching.

This is not to say that the struggle over Aristotle had been an easy one for the masters of the Faculty of Arts at the University of Paris. Not at all. Aligned against them were the masters of theology, who objected to the continuous cry of philosophers of the arts faculty who demanded that reason be thought of greater account than faith, revelation, or the standard Church authorities. Even the king sided with the bishop of Paris, and the masters of theology aligned against the Faculty of Arts and its pagan philosophers. When the students, who enjoyed the philosophic disputations and the use of Aristotelian logic, rioted in 1229, the king sent soldiers to quell the riot. Only the intervention of the pope preserved the independence of both students and masters of arts.

As it became almost standard practice to consider the period of transition the "Dark Ages," and to ascribe dogmatism and intellectual backwardness to the Middle Ages, so Aristotle has been portrayed as the intellectual master to the Middle Ages, finally overthrown by the "new science," led by Galileo. It is misleading to assert that Aristotelian logic became ossified in the sterile dialect of something called Scholasticism, and constituted a roadblock to science that had to be blasted away by Roger Bacon, Francis Bacon, Galileo, Kepler, and their allies.

There was a genuine issue surrounding the limits on certification of knowledge by authority. The medieval Church faced religious heresies and assertions of secular power by kings, Christian and foreign. Naturally enough, it sought to preserve and assert the authority of faith in every possible way, especially in matters of faith and morals. This made for rigidity of doctrine and intolerance, although there was no lack of free inquiry into theological, as well as philosophical questions, nor did the inquiry have to wait till the thirteenth century. As early as the ninth century John the Scot (c. 810-875), known as Erigena, applied logical analysis to the most touchy theological questions.

Boethius (c. 480-524) had provided the Middle Ages with a portion of Aristotle's logic, materials with which Gerbert of Rheims, toward the end of the tenth century, was able to use in launching a revival of Aristotelian logic (19:175-176). The Church did not stand in Gerbert's way. "Logic," Gerbert wrote while at Chartres, "opened a window on to an orderly and systematic view of the world and of man's mind" (19:180). Though the masters of theology were to be anxious about this revival, John the Scot and Gerbert were showing the value of *reason*, preparing the way for the later conclusion of the highest Church authorities that there cannot be a conflict of faith (authority) with reason.

The way to this happy resolution was not easy. The Church fought for faith over reason, and at times could not be certain even of survival. But its leaders did learn that Aristotelian logic would not undermine faith, that it actually could be used to combat intellectual heresy sponsored by Moslem philosophers. If anything, Aristotelian logic came to be too fondly embraced. At first, in the eleventh century, it was needed, as Gerbert wrote, to create an "orderly and systematic view of the world and of man's mind." Thus the student at the cathedral school of Chartres was set to studying Porphyry's *Introduction* to Aristotle and Boethius' commentary on Aristotle (19). Had Southern (19) not limited himself to the dawn of the Middle Ages he would have remarked, as did Van Steenberghen (21), that by the middle of the thirteenth century the students of the University of Paris had become ✻ wildly enthusiastic about Aristotelian analysis.

Though the history of education should not be written simply in terms of leading figures, the tremendous success Aristotelian logic finally attained at the University of Paris was the peculiar achievement of a single man, Peter Abelard (1079-1142), perhaps better remembered for his tragic love ✓ affair with Héloïse. Abelard had been a student at the cathedral school of Notre Dame in Paris. Later, as the best-known master in Paris, Abelard won a place in theological study for Aristotelian logic, and ". . . fixed once and for all the characteristics of the scholastic method, thereby settling decisively the direction which speculative theology was to take" (21:34). By training his students in Aristotelian logical analysis, Abelard helped to ✗ turn theology from *citing* authorities to *interpreting* Scripture. Not all of his theological colleagues followed suit, but the defenders of the strict authority of faith ultimately lost ground before the increasing popularity of defending faith with the sword of Aristotle's logic (21:39).

The systematization of experience that Aristotle's *Categories* permitted ✓ in the early Middle Ages was overdone in the thirteenth, fourteenth, and fifteenth centuries. This was the reason for the vehemence with which scholasticism has been held up to scorn, not only in the Renaissance but by non-Catholic philosophers ever since. The scorn in part was merited; many medieval philosophers were "logic choppers" (*nugiloqui ventilatores*) who debated endlessly, collecting differing opinions of authorities without questioning whether the opinions were authoritative. Roger Bacon (*c.* 1214-1292) could accept Scripture as a supreme source of wisdom, but if a question was raised about "How many Angels could stand on the head of a pin," Bacon insisted that no answer was to be found either in the Scriptures or in the authorities favored by the majority of theologians or—and this was crucial—in some statement such as: "It is *self-evident* that. . . ." Bacon had studied too long with Robert Grosseteste, later to be Bishop of Lincoln, England, to believe that many things were self-evident. He would have granted that Aristotle was correct in saying that a thing could not both be and not be at the same time; this principle, which Aristotle called the prin- ✓ ciple of self-contradiction, made sense to experimentalists like Grosseteste and Bacon. But they felt that it would take a great deal of experimentation to find out about nature; deducing the characteristics of nature from self-evident principles impressed them as most unprofitable.

> Among the first to understand and use the new theory of experimental science . . . the real founder of the tradition of scientific thought in medieval Oxford and, in some ways, of the modern English intellectual tradition, Grosseteste united in his own work the experimental and rational traditions of the twelfth century and he set forth a systematic theory of experimental science (6:219).

Robert Grosseteste (1168-1253) may have been first chancellor of Oxford University; he was a leading figure at Oxford when the "general strike" at the University of Paris in 1229 brought a great many masters and students from Paris. At any rate, Grosseteste knew of the struggle at Oxford between the Faculties of Philosophy and Theology.

A conservative in theology, Grosseteste believed that Biblical texts were the only basis for theological statement (21:133). Grosseteste was a radical in philosophy, however. For ten years (199-1209), he taught in the arts faculty, concentrating his teaching in Aristotelian logic. Grosseteste not only knew Aristotle's works, but he knew both the Arabic commentaries on Aristotle *and* the Arabian publications on science that had been stimulated by Arab study of Aristotle. These writings apparently captured his fancy, for though he wrote on philosophy in general, his mark was made in the Middle Ages in his sponsorship of experimental science.

One might say that Grosseteste was a sceptic. He wanted convincing explanations for anything asserted to be true. It was not enough to say to him: "It is God's will." This also had not been enough of an answer for another Englishman, Adelard of Bath, who had insisted that the study of how things in nature happened ("natural causes") were legitimate subjects of inquiry (6:11-12). Grosseteste was not satisfied that the inquiry had gone far enough if it was demonstrated that the phenomenon observed could be deduced from some principle or axiom. He continued to ask "why?" even of such axioms as "a straight line is the shortest distance between two points. . . ." The Greeks had been satisfied that Euclidean-type principles were indemonstrable or self-evident, but Grosseteste asked *how a thoughtful person arrived at self-evident principles.* The Greeks and the later rationalists were much more taken with what could be concluded or deduced from general, *self-evident* principles than they were in exploring nature to see what principles might be *found,* by experiment and observation, to be generally true. Grosseteste had revived that portion of Greek Sophism which asked after the nature or causes of things. An anti-sceptical, anti-experimental reaction might have been anticipated, but to look for that opposition would be to anticipate the hardships of Galileo in the seventeenth century.

1. ATKINS, J. W. H., *English Literary Criticism: The Medieval Phase.* New York: Cambridge University Press, 1943.

2. BALDWIN, CHARLES S., *Medieval Rhetoric and Poetic.* New York: The Macmillan Company, 1928.

3. BARKER, ERNEST, GEORGE CLARK, and P. VAUCHER, eds., *The European Inheritance,* Vol. I. Oxford: The Clarendon Press, 1954.

4. BOYD, WILLIAM, *The History of Western Education.* London: A. & C. Black, Ltd., 1952.

5. BROWNE, G. F., *Alcuin of York.* London: Society for Promoting Christian Knowledge, 1908.

6. CROMBIE, A. C., *Augustine to Galileo: The History of Science A.D. 400-1650.* Cambridge, Mass.: Harvard University Press, 1953.

7. ———, *Robert Grosseteste and the Origins of Experimental Science: 1100-1700.* Oxford: The Clarendon Press, 1953.

8. EBY, FREDERICK and CHARLES F. ARROWOOD, *The History and Philosophy of Education, Ancient and Medieval.* Englewood Cliffs, N. J.: Prentice-Hall, Inc., 1940.

9. HASKINS, CHARLES H., *The Rise of Universities.* Gloucester, Mass.: Peter Smith, 1940.

10. HEALY, JOHN, *Ireland's Ancient Schools and Scholars.* Dublin: Sealy, Bryers, and Walker, 1902.

11. LEACH, A. F., *The Schools of Medieval England.* London: Methuen and Co., Ltd., 1915.

12. LOPEZ, ROBERT S., "The Trade of Medieval Europe: The South," *The Cambridge Economic History of Europe,* Vol. II, ed. by M. Postan and E. E. Rich. New York: Cambridge University Press, 1952.

13. MCKEON, RICHARD, "Rhetoric in the Middle Ages," *Speculum,* XVII, No. 1 (1942), 1-32.

14. MCLAUGHLIN, MARY M., "Paris Masters of the Thirteenth and Fourteenth Centuries and Ideas of Intellectual Freedom," *Church History,* XXIV, No. 3 (1955), 195-211.

15. MUNDY, JOHN H. and PETER RIESENBERG, *The Medieval Town.* Princeton: D. Van Nostrand Co., Inc., 1958.

16. POSTAN, MICHAEL, "The Trade of Medieval Europe: The North" in *The Cambridge Economic History of Europe,* Vol. II, ed. by M. Postan and E. E. Rich. New York: Cambridge University Press, 1952.

17. RASHDALL, HASTINGS, *The Universities of Europe in the Middle Ages,* ed. by F. M. Powicke and A. B. Emden, 3 vols. Oxford: The Clarendon Press, 1936.

18. SHEPHERD, WILLIAM R., *Historical Atlas.* Pikesville, Md.: The Colonial Offset Co., Inc., 1956.

19. SOUTHERN, E. W., *The Making of the Middle Ages.* New Haven: Yale University Press, 1959.

20. THOMPSON, JAMES W., *The Literacy of the Laity in the Middle Ages*. New York: Burt Franklin, 1960.

21. VAN STEENBERGHEN, FERNAND, *Aristotle in the West*, tr. by L. Johnston. Louvain: E. Nauwelaerts, Publisher, 1955.

22. WALBANK, FRANK W., "Trade and Industry under the Later Roman Empire in the West," *The Cambridge Economic History of Europe*, Vol. II, ed. by M. Postan and E. E. Rich. New York: Cambridge University Press, 1952.

23. WEST, ANDREW F., *Alcuin and the Rise of the Christian Schools*. New York: Charles Scribner's Sons, 1899.

24. WHITE, T. H., *The Bestiary: A Book of Beasts*. New York: G. P. Putnam's Sons, 1960.

The fifteenth, sixteenth, and seventeenth centuries saw astonishing growth in the population of western Europe. Europe literally outgrew its borders and, like ancient Greece, sent colonists abroad. France, Spain, Portugal, Holland, and England all possessed colonies by 1650. In the English colonies dotting the eastern seaboard of the New World, first steps were taken toward public education. For the Puritans of Massachusetts Bay, education was a vital portion of their religion; illiterate men could not read the Gospels and Protestantism demanded that each man read and know the Scriptures. Before the era discussed in this chapter ended, the New World had come to be a remarkable reflection of the Old. Mercantilism—an association of private commerce with national government— created the Massachusetts Bay Colony; a royal charter for settlement and exploitation of the area was granted the group who became the Massachusetts colonists. The ambitions of the Spanish court financed Columbus. French monarchs were not indifferent to French traders on the Mississippi or in the Louisiana Territory, which bore the stamp of

47

EDUCATION, NATIONALISM, RELIGION, AND HUMANISM: 1400-1700

4

the imperial title of the Louises. As the mother nations fought in Europe and on the seas, so they fought for colonial territories, which they expected to supply raw materials and to which they proposed to send and sell finished products. The English colonists in the New World became pawns in the nationalistic struggles for wealth and power between England and France, and in the end Mother England was to find that colonial merchants did not intend to supply either manpower with which to fight the French, raw materials to furnish English workshops, or the money to purchase goods made in England.

Educators were not untouched by the affairs of Empire. When Henry VIII came to the throne of England in 1509, he lost no time in allying himself with the power of Spain by marrying Catherine of Aragon, by whom he had a daughter, Mary. A leading Spanish humanist, Juan Luis Vives, while visiting with his English humanist friends, was befriended by the Queen of England and engaged as tutor for the Princess Mary. Vives (1492-1540) was one of the most able scholars of the time, and for twenty years he lived at the court of Henry as royal tutor until in 1529 Henry decided to divorce Catherine. Vives was discharged when he took the side of the Catholic queen in Henry's suit for divorce, and he left England for Belgium.

Education and educators were hurt by religious intolerance, which knew no forebearance. Though no scholar of this period outshone Desiderius Erasmus, a Catholic and truly a man-of-the-world, not even he was spared. The writings of Erasmus were known throughout Europe; he was an intimate of the chief intellectual circle of England during his stays there. A scholarly reputation and abstention from politics did not, however, shield him from religious intolerance. In 1521 Erasmus had to leave Louvain, Belgium, because of religious controversy, and his last years in Switzerland were saddened by bitter criticisms of him, not only by Calvinists who detested him as a Catholic, but also by Catholics who resented the sarcasm with which he pressed for higher intellectual and spiritual standards to guide Catholic churchmen.

Histories that have dealt with education during the latter half of the sixteenth century and all of the seventeenth have been less than faithful to reality in minimizing the hazards to which any number of educators were exposed in these years of unrestrained religious strife. Peter Ramus (1515-1572), whose work has yet to receive its due (11:vii), was driven into exile in 1562 and again in 1567. With him went thousands of other French Huguenot Protestants. In the savage massacre of St. Bartholomew's Day (August 23-24, 1572), Ramus was killed (11:12-13). The Edict of Nantes (1598) presumably granted the French Protestants religious freedom, but there was no end in France to bitter religious controversy involving educators.

Doubtless the most moving ordeal was that undergone by Comenius

(1592-1670), bishop of a Protestant sect known as the Moravian Brethren. In his day, Comenius had few distinguished rivals among the other educators. His textbook on Latin grammar, *The Door of the Languages Unlocked,* became a favorite, and was translated from Czech into twelve European and four Asiatic languages. With subsequent writings his reputation became greater until important Englishmen persuaded Parliament to invite Comenius to establish his ideal university of "pansophic" or universal knowledge. The English Civil War of 1642 prevented the plan from coming to fruition, and Comenius went off to Sweden with the hope of creating a pansophic university there. What is less well known is that those who managed the affairs of Harvard College had invited Comenius, while he was living in Holland, to become president of Harvard after the resignation of President Dunster in 1654.

The Reformation only divided Western Christendom into Roman Catholic and Protestant folds; European civilization remained Christian. The supreme importance for a good and eternal life attributed to Christianity in Europe held true as much for the Renaissance in the fifteenth century as for the sixteenth and seventeenth centuries. For educators, the preeminence of Christianity meant that even Greek and Roman authors, to whom all wisdom was attributed, could be accepted as excellent resources for the preparation of Christians. The classic languages—Hebrew, Greek, and Latin—were praised as the tongues that had to be learned if the early texts of the Scriptures were to be read. Even the scruples of the most moral Christian preachers seemed to have been allayed. "To the Greeks we are indebted for everything," wrote Alexander Hegius, devout Catholic rector of the renowned school of the Brethren of the Common Life in the Dutch market town of Deventer (3:172). In the same vein as Hegius, Sturm, a Protestant, wrote that the objective of education was a "wise and eloquent piety" (*sapiens et eloquens pietas*); "lettered piety" (*pietas literata*) was the more common phrase employed by Protestants to describe the objective of education. Religiously stern Puritans, while they murmured about some of the "pagan" elements of the Greek and Roman classics ". . . found it easy to reconcile themselves to the established practice of regarding the ancient languages as a key to the word of God. This view showed itself most plainly in the characterization of Latin, Greek, and Hebrew as 'holy languages,' and in the occasional use of the New Testament in beginning the study of Latin and Greek" (3:231).

Four centuries earlier, during the Middle Ages, Christian objections to pagan literature were strong and not infrequently heard, but the objection was not to learning and using classic languages, especially Latin. "How," asked Honorius of Auton, "is the soul to be profited by the strife of Hector, the arguments of Plato, the poems of Virgil or the elegies of Ovid?" If Honorius was one of the more conservative of medieval intellectuals, his views were shared by the very independent Abelard (1079-1142), devoted to Aristotle, who asked why bishops did not "expel from the city of God those poets whom Plato forbade to enter into his city of the world."

Later, in the fifteenth century, Giovanni Dominici, Friar of Santa Maria Novella in Florence, refused to admit a reconciliation of the antique with the Christian spirit, nor would his colleague of the same church, that fierce preacher against impiety, Savonarola (23:39). For both Dominici and Savonarola, there was obvious opposition between the Renaissance craving for fame (*gloria*), the worship of "individuality, personal force and self-assertion," and the Christian virtues of humility, self-repression, and surrender to external will. Persuasive as was the fiery Savonarola, the "humanists" prevailed.

Although the humanists withheld credit for the revival of classic languages from their medieval predecessors, the time of the humanist victory found great numbers of Latin manuscripts, if not the Greek originals, in cathedrals and monasteries. The *Scriptoria* of the monks had done their work. Greek as well as Latin now were safely secured as the prime languages of learning; it only remained to save Hebrew. The honor of rescuing and preserving Hebrew in the Renaissance goes to Reuchlin, a leading friend of academic freedom during the second half of the Renaissance.

CHRISTIAN, WORLDLY, AND PROMETHEAN HUMANISM

In the eighteenth, nineteenth, and into the twentieth century, there have been humanists who have been attached to no church. In this sense, humanism has meant a devotion to the potentialities of human reason unsupported by supernatural power. In the fifteenth, sixteenth, and seventeenth centuries it would be difficult to conceive of any humanist who would draw a line between his humanism and his Christianity. There were some humanists, however, who were more worldly than Erasmus—to name a most Christian humanist. John Locke (1632-1704) was more worldly than Erasmus, but only in the sense that his writing on education was aimed at tutoring those who were to be the aristocrats and leaders of society. Erasmus was slightly more occupied with having young people master the "holy" languages that would permit an intimate knowledge of the Graeco-Roman world, in which lay the foundations of Christianity.

There were humanists less taken with unlocking Scripture with the key of its ancient languages than they were in reading Greek and Roman texts for knowledge of the order of nature and government. Such a man was Rabelais (1495-1553), a priest, to be sure, but better known as the physician and satirist who mocked medieval philosophers in order to praise the "new science." For Rabelais there was a storehouse of scientific knowledge in

Greek and Latin, and he was more eager to explore it than the scriptural. For this it was necessary to learn the classic languages and literature.

The differences between Erasmus and Rabelais were real, but despite them, in all essentials, the educational programs recommended by Erasmus and Rabelais agreed. To distinguish between their ultimate objectives it would be well to think of Erasmus as a *Christian* humanist and Rabelais as a *Promethean* humanist. For the latter, the knowledge of the ancients becomes a powerful tool for improving the future of mankind.

There would be no merit in compounding types of humanism beyond the Christian, the worldly, and the Promethean; these three were the chief categories of humanism till the French Revolution. It would be a mistake also to exaggerate their different emphases, for they were no more than emphases. Humanism was the theme; Christian, worldly, and Promethean humanism were variations—the Christian and Promethean perhaps further apart than the worldly humanism from either of them. Perhaps the common ground is evident from the fact that these humanists knew each other. For example, Loyola (founder of the Jesuit order) was a student at the University of Paris at the same time as were Calvin and Erasmus. Vives, the Spanish humanist, was a friend of Erasmus and of the English friends of Erasmus, principally Sir Thomas More. Not infrequently the humanists taught, or were students, in the same schools at some time during their lives. The humanist schools of the Brethren of the Common Life most frequently played host to humanist students and teachers. Hegius was Rector (1465-1498) of the School of the Brethren of the Common Life in Deventer, Holland, when Erasmus was in attendance as a boy. At another school of the Brethren, one in Liége, Belgium, John Sturm was a pupil, and later used the organization of this school as a model for his own influential gymnasium (grammar school) in Strassburg, Germany. Sturm's gymnasium, incidentally, was the forerunner of the Latin school that became the pride of German education until World War II. In the sixteenth century its fame already was assured; Calvin came to Sturm's school as a teacher and patterned all his formal recommendations for education on the Strassburg plan. In this manner, the conception of schooling evolved by Alexander Hegius was used by Sturm and Calvin and left as a legacy for later centuries, not only in Germany, but in England, Scotland, and the North American colonies.

51

THE HUMANIST CORE IN ALL VARIATIONS OF PRACTICE AND THEORY

Devotion to the educational theory of Quintilian and Plutarch (c. A.D. 46-120). For guidance in educational theory, the period looked to Quintilian and Plutarch, a contemporary of Quintilian. The names of both Romans, with Quintilian leading, appear again and again. Plutarch's *On the Education of Children* was translated from the Greek in 1411 by Guarino da

Verona. An Italian humanist, Poggio, chanced upon the manuscript copy of Quintilian's *Institutio oratoria* in 1416; the text of Cicero's *De oratore* came to light in Lodi, Italy, six years later. Of the three, Quintilian's *Institutes* became the most influential, Erasmus excusing his failure to write more on the aim and method of teaching by saying that it was unnecessary, "seeing that Quintilian has said the last word on that matter."

There was a fondness for quotation, and Quintilian and Plutarch are the authors of almost all the quotations in that model for humanists, the quotation-laden essay on education that took the form of a letter from Aeneas Silvio (1405-1464), later Pope Pius II, written as advice for the education of the young Ladislaus, King of Hungary and Bohemia (18). From both Plutarch and Quintilian the humanists accepted the Hellenic idea that youth should be set models for character and correct expression. Not unexpectedly, humanist writing for the young tended to be a recital of advice on deportment and wisdom as offered by both early Christian and pagan authors.

Further, the primacy of memory was endorsed; Plutarch and Quintilian had praised memory above all mental faculties, believing that when young people remembered examples of correct conduct and expression they would use them. "A good memory," wrote Quintilian, "is the first sign of good native intelligence" (*prium ingenii signum*). Plutarch, whose *Lives of Famous Men* was a textbook for humanist educators, agreed with his colleague. In his *On the Education of Children*, Plutarch wrote, "Above everything else, it is important to train and exercise the memory of the young, since it is the storehouse of education."

As followers of Quintilian, the humanists, almost to a man, accepted Quintilian's dictate that children never were to be beaten, that all instruction was to be made interesting, that the maturity and interests of the student were to be studied by the teacher and used rather than ignored. However often these precepts of Quintilian were ignored in practice, the humanist educators endorsed them without reservation. The cruel practices of schools in the eighteenth and nineteenth centuries only attested that their directors and teachers were ignorant of the humanist preachments of the three centuries preceding.

The importance of learning Latin and its grammar. Although a student at Harvard in the seventeenth century was expected to learn Hebrew, it was only the Protestant most anxious to read the Old Testament in the original who insisted on a place for Hebrew in the curriculum, and then, only in higher education. Greek was more widely sponsored, but almost always the first language to be learned was Latin, with Greek introduced after four years of schooling. There was no rivalry in the matter; no humanist disputed the first place of Latin as the language of the Church fathers. The Protestant leaders of the sixteenth century, for the most part, had been Catholic, brought up with Latin. Men like Calvin and Luther, tremendously concerned with reading the oldest manuscripts of what was known as the New Testament, would have had to be able to read Greek. But there were Latin translations which were trustworthy, and Latin translations could be made.

It was only Luther's undertaking to publish a German, vernacular, translation of the Bible that caught the eye of historians. In Luther's use of German was the portent of *universal* schooling. *All children would have to be taught German if the German translation of Scripture was to have any meaning.* Luther intended his translation of the Bible into German to be more than a gesture. Each Protestant leader had the same intention, of instructing the masses at least in their vernacular language, and in the vernacular version of some portion of Scripture and religious teaching.

Although the Protestant Reformation helped to speed the time when education—elementary schooling first—would be in the native tongue, no humanist educator fought for enlarging the role of vernacular languages. Erasmus was quite typical of the humanists in stating flatly that he would abstain from the use of the vernacular languages (23:62). He knew Dutch, of course, having been brought up in Holland, but in his visits to England most of his conversations were in Latin. "The popular speech," he wrote, "has, and ought to have, no claim to be regarded as a fit instrument of literary expression" (23:63). And the French humanist Montaigne (1533-1592) remarked that he felt more at home in Latin than in French. "To me, Latin is, as it were, natural; I understand it better than French."

Erasmus and Montaigne, while they carried the day for Latin, were not the only side heard. In France in the late seventeenth century there was Coustel, one of the most able teachers associated with the celebrated Catholic schools, the Little Schools of Port Royal, operated from about 1646-1660 by the Port Royalists (3:256-261). Coustel's *Rules for the Education of Children* (1687) comprises a comprehensive account of the principles of this influential order, one of which was to teach children to appreciate and use their mother tongue, French. Coustel's praise of French parallels Mulcaster's (c. 1530-1611) praise of English as "of itself both deep in conceit and frank in delivery" (3:232-233). Mulcaster was unusual among English headmasters, however, especially when one recalls that he was headmaster for twenty-five years at the Latin grammar school, Merchant Taylor's, and St. Paul's School, whose headmaster had once been Lily, author of one of most widely used Latin grammars of the age of humanism.

Despite Mulcaster and Coustel, the humanists threw their weight behind Latin and established the prestige of Latin for three hundred years, at least in European secondary schooling. Even in colonial America and later in the United States, Latin was not unseated despite the efforts of Benjamin Franklin. But Franklin's duel with the Latinists belonged to a later period. For the fifteenth, sixteenth, and seventeenth centuries—the time of humanism with a capital "H"—the more lively issue was whether Latin and Greek were to be taught for the content of their literature or in order to perfect eloquence, as represented by Cicero the orator. Those who advocated the latter became known as Ciceronians.

The honor of first presenting the Western world with a comprehensive humanist view of education belongs to Pietro Paolo Vergerio (1349-1420), who revived for his successors throughout the Renaissance the writings of Quintilian on education. But Vergerio did more. His *On the Manners of a Gentleman and on Liberal Studies* bears a typically worldly humanist title; John Locke (1632-1704) could have written under just that title in seventeenth century England, Montaigne (1533-1592) could have used the title in France, and it would have fitted also the tutorial task of Fénelon (1651-1715). Vergerio wrote his treatise for the guidance of the son of a lord of the Italian city of Padua, and in no essential did it differ from either Quintilian or Plutarch; it is the same as that advice given young King Ladislaus of Hungary and Bohemia in the long letter from Aeneas Silvio.

But the man who brought all the educational hopes of the early Renaissance to realization in a school was the truly splendid intellect Vittorino da Feltre (1378-1446). Vittorino did not escape the necessary limitation of all humanists before contemporary times—that of recommending schooling that fitted only those who had the leisure of wealth and the responsibilities of aristocracy. But Vittorino's aristocracy was to be an *active* aristocracy, genuinely leading in intellectual, economic, political, and military affairs, as well as more social affairs. A further limitation to Vittorino's thought was his failure to include scientific studies in the curriculum, though he was one of the better mathematicians of his day; he has thus handed on to contemporary humanists the problem of finding a place in education for the practical and scientific, and it must be admitted that they have not done well in managing the problem, despite their vantage of more than half a millennium of history.

Vittorino spent twenty-three years as a tutor in the employ of an Italian nobleman, Gianfrancesco Gonzaga, Lord of Mantua, in the pay of Venice. Gonzaga accomplished almost nothing that is recorded, beyond displaying the wisdom of employing Vittorino. Gonzaga's title was not "legitimate"; that is, it had not been inherited. To develop a reputation he, and other noblemen like him, hired such men as Vittorino. The lord of Carra hired Giovanni Conversino da Ravenna and Vergerio. The D'estes—whose estates annually attract thousands of tourists in Italy—engaged as tutors both Guarino and Gaza, the former having published the manuscript the newly discovered *On the Education of Children* by Plutarch. Vittorino's own teacher of Latin, the eminent Barzizza, was in private employ as was Chrysoloras, who had come from Constantinople as the first public teacher of Greek in Italy.

Vittorino stands as an example of the best-educated worldly and Christian humanist; he had too little knowledge of science to be considered Promethean. His own elementary and secondary schooling was in the *trivium* and *quadrivium*. At eighteen, Vittorino entered the University of Padua, there to study rhetoric with Barzizza and Giovanni da Ravenna—who had spent years as a famulus and pupil in the home of Petrarch, the first poet and literary critic to use the Italian vernacular. Vittorina had learned a good deal of mathematics, but at Padua he definitely turned to the typically humanistic studies, joining the faculty as a Master of Latin Grammar. Following an interlude in which he studied Greek with Guarino at Venice, Vittorino returned to Padua and succeeded Barzizza as Master of Rhetoric. The students at the university were too rowdy for him, however, and he left Padua for the employ of Gonzaga, converting a summer house on the estate into a school. The temper of that school can be read out of the name Vittorino gave it. Gonzaga, for good reason, had called his summer house *La Giosa* (the Pleasure House). Vittorino slightly altered the name—to make it rather more proper for a school—to *La Giocasa* (The Pleasant House). He intended that instruction be pleasant, even as Quintilian had directed.

55

The pleasantness of La Giocasa rested in the manner of Vittorino—as well as in the physical location of the villa, for there was nothing easy about the course of study. Had not Quintilian said that memory was the first sign of intelligence? Had not Plutarch firmly pronounced on the importance of stocking the memory of the young? A well-furnished memory had to be put to use in rhetoric, a use approved by Quintilian and Cicero, both "professors" of rhetoric and oratory, as Vittorino had been himself. The students learned to be eloquent with their Latin learning.

La Giocasa became the leading school of the fifteenth century. Nicholas Perotti, whose Latin grammar was to be used by Erasmus as a standard text, taught there. Valla had preceded Perotti, and like him was a student of Latin grammar, having published a grammar that displaced the medieval grammars—that of Alexander de Villa Dei, for example. George of Trebizond also taught at La Giocasa, and on leaving published a book on rhetorical style that led the field. Theodore Gaza had a place on Vittorino's staff; his grammar was the companion of Perotti's in the classrooms of Erasmus. At least three of the leading humanists of the day—Guarino, Filelfo, and Poggio—had sons enrolled with Vittorino. Perhaps no schoolman after Isocrates, Plato, and Aristotle has had a reputation comparable to that of Vittorino.

Instruction at La Giocasa began early in the morning and early in a child's life. Quintilian had surmised that three or four years of age was a good time to begin schooling, and Vittorino admitted children to La Giocasa at four or five. The primary classes worked with the three R's, drawing (which had been added to early education during Hellenistic times), and the elements of religious instruction—at least memorization of the Psalms, the Creed, the Lord's Prayer, and the Hymn to the Virgin. Keenly concerned with the moral tone of La Giocasa, Vitorrino introduced "character education" through commentary on Greek and Roman myths, Plutarch's *Fables*, and biographies of outstanding religious figures.

The three R's having been mastered, or on their way to being mastered, Perotti or Valla would give the children a simple Latin grammar, composed on the premises. The difficulty of Latin for such young students was not as overwhelming as might be imagined. The older children spoke Latin and the youngsters heard it all the time. Nor was Latin a foreign language to the Italian ear. Ability to read readied the student for his next task, careful training in declamation and eloquence.

CICERONIANISM, GRAMMAR, AND SPECIALIZATION

The humanists must be seen as *generalists* rather than specialists. As John Milton (1608-1674) defined the humanist aim in education, it was to provide a "complete and generous Education." "I call . . . a complete and generous Education that which fits a man to perform justly, skillfully and magnanimously all the offices both private and public of peace and war" (6:9). There was no narrowness in that intention, although by Milton's time humanism had begun to suffer from specialization, both in Latin grammar and in a pursuit of a Ciceronian style in eloquence. Though Milton himself struggled against the specialists as Erasmus had before him, the broad, general education that would have won the approval of Isocrates, or Cicero for that matter, was modified by those who took a much more narrow view of education. Chief among the latter was John Sturm (1507-1589), the year of whose birth was the centennial of Barzizza's assumption of the chair of Latin and rhetoric at the University of Padua, an event that may have marked the inception of Ciceronianism.

Even Guarino, who had taught Vittorino his Greek and had sent his own son to school at La Giocasa with Vittorino, moved away from the conception of education as preparation for all phases of life. Vittorino had followed the Hellenic prescription, including sports, games, exercise at La Giocasa, and he was mindful of the careers his pupils would follow. If he felt that young Frederigo of Urbino was destined to follow a career in arms (a likely prospect), Vittorino hoped that the program at La Giocasa would help him. For Guarino, wrote Boyd, ". . . instruction in the classical literatures was . . . an end in itself instead of simply a means to the all-round development of the good man" (3:166). And Guarino's son, despite the broad goals Vittorino held for La Giocasa, graduated from Vittorino's school to write *On the Method of Teaching and of Reading the Classical Authors*, in which the young Guarino placed more emphasis on the form (or methods) of instruction than on what was to be taught or expected by way of response from the students. More indicative of what was to come was the specialization inherent in his sentence: "The foundation of education must be laid in grammar" (3:166-167).

What had happened was that tremendous enthusiasm engendered in Italy for the classical tradition, which suddenly was recognized as *their* tradition, had led to imitating every detail of the form of expression that had been used by those who were held the best of their forebears (7), and of these Cicero had carried off the honors. As Woodward put it, the Italian humanists of the fifteenth century treated ancient Rome as the "living heritage of their nation" (23:31). The golden age for the "cult of imitation," as Baldwin terms it, was Augustan Rome, and loud were the demands that there be conformity in the teaching of Latin according to "Augustan diction." Baldwin reminds his readers that Lorenzo Valla's *Elegantiae linguae latinae* (1476) was "reprinted again and again, first of a long line of phrase books, and characteristic of its very title, as a guide to conformity" (5:19). Conformity in the Latin used in the schools meant a good deal in the heyday of humanism in Europe, for all instruction at the secondary or high school level was in Latin.

57

The Ciceronians carried their point to the extreme. Bembo, one of the better known Italian grammarians of the fifteenth century, refused to use any words or idioms other than those employed by Cicero. He even insisted on using pagan Latin terms in writing of Christian ideas and personalities. The Virgin Mary he referred to as *dea ipsa* (this goddess) and nuns became *virgines vestale* (vestal virgins) (3:168). But Bembo was not an oddity. By 1510, all of Europe was caught up in intense debate about what constituted correct Latin expression in writing and in speech. Was it Cicero who was to be the model or was it Tacitus or, perhaps, Livy? Nations took sides; Germans were ranged against French and Italian scholars, but those who argued did not question that one of the Latin greats should furnish the style of contemporary language. The imitators were riding high. It was at this point, in the 1520's, that Erasmus felt called upon to enter the discussion, and despite his own devotion to Latin, to rebuke the Ciceronians. His essay, the *Dialogus Ciceronianus* (1527-28) posed the central thesis. "Times have changed," he argued, "our instincts, needs, ideas, are not those of Cicero. Let us indeed take example from him. He was a borrower, an imitator, if you will; but he copied in order to assimilate, to bring what he found into the service of his own age" (23:53).

But Erasmus, power among intellectuals though he was, was unable to provide a sufficient countervailing force to the Ciceronians. Had he persuaded the Ciceronians, humanism might have remained alive as a force in education. But Erasmus failed, and the humanistic studies came to mean increasing attention to grammar and style—to form rather than content.

BIBLIOGRAPHY

See the references at the end of Chapter 5.

In all of northern Europe—though not
necessarily in England—preoccupation with the
grammar and style of the Ciceronian Latin really
shaped academic education for centuries. After all,
Ciceronians operated the schools that later
schoolmen copied. Though these Ciceronians did
not write books on education, they had schools
to show visitors eager to find models for the
schools they, too, wished to open; anti-
Ciceronians wrote essays, but the Ciceronians had
the schools. Even if someone responsible for
organizing a school had been moved by what
Rabelais wrote against the Ciceronians, he could
not look to Rabelais for practical guidance, for
Rabelais operated no school in which his theories
could be seen to live. The same was true of
Montaigne and Locke. The point has been overlooked that for a schoolmaster saddled with the
difficult responsibility of organizing a school, it
was interesting to read the essays against
Ciceronianism, but seeing a school that seemed
to be a success was far more persuasive. The
educators emphasizing Latin grammar and style

59

EDUCATION, HUMANISM, AND THE NEW SCIENCE: 1400-1700

5

had the schools. Even essayists as persuasive as Erasmus or Montaigne could do no more than urge their colleagues to spare students too many grammatical rules. Erasmus could complain about the Ciceronianism of his own schooling in Deventer, in the school of the Brethren of the Common Life, but he could not and did not succeed in slowing the spread of those schools and others modeled after them.

Sturm's (1507-1589) gymnasium represented the schooling of the latter portion of the humanistic period, just as Vittorino's La Giocasa represented the earlier Renaissance. For some historians, Vittorino stood for humanism, or the Renaissance in southern Europe, while Sturm, along with Montaigne, Rabelais, Erasmus, Comenius, Mulcaster, Milton, and Locke have been cast as "educators of North Europe." This geographical distinction never had validity; humanism ignored geographical boundaries and even the distinction between the *Catholic* South and the *Protestant* North. When it came to educational theory and practice, one would be hard put to distinguish between the Protestant Sturm—friend of Melanchthon and Luther—and a prominent Catholic humanist selected for contrast.

True, for primary education the Protestant would have been more, much more, interested in having *all* children learn the vernacular language in order to insure their being able to read the Scriptures and catechisms written in the vernacular. Like the Puritans of the Massachusetts Bay Colony, who published court orders in 1642 and 1647 calling for primary schools and where there was sufficient population, for grammar or secondary schools, Protestant educators were aware of the fact that the great bulk of the population would not continue their schooling long enough to learn or need Latin. However, for the students who were thought to be the future leaders in Church, state, commerce, or education, there was no difference between southern or northern humanists, Catholic or Protestant. And for the humanist who wished to have a school, Sturm's would have furnished a handy model.

Equally to the point, many of the leading humanists knew each other personally, or were well-acquainted with each other's writings. Like their medieval forerunners, the humanists were cosmopolitan. Their common possession of Latin meant that there was no barrier to communication among them. They were men of the world—in that sense they were worldly humanists, as well as in the sense of preparing students for the life they might be expected to lead. There is another sense in which a humanist was a man of the world; he belonged not to any single nation of men but to humanity. As Woodward wrote to Erasmus: ". . . he longs in his heart for a republic of enlightenment which knowing no country shall be coterminous with humanity" (3:35). Erasmus himself asked men to ask "not where, but how nobly we spend our lives. . . . Love of fatherland is good, but it is more philosophic to regard things and human beings in such a way that this world may be looked upon as the common fatherland of all . . . I wish to be a citizen of the whole world, not of a single city" (3:65). This was one of the successful statements of a humanist aware of his association with humanity.

Sturm's background was typical of the development of humanistic education throughout the Renaissance. He had been a pupil at a school of the Brethren of the Common Life operating in the Belgian city of Liége. The school had been open since 1496 when societies of the Brethren (and Sisters) of the Common Life were some one hundred and twenty years old, having been initiated in about 1376 by Geert Groot of Deventer. Groot had been disturbed at the immoral influences to which young people were subject in the great market town of Deventer. Erasmus and Sturm were only two graduates of these schools to become famous as intellectuals and educators. In northern Europe in the sixteenth century, apparently almost all the distinguished scholars and teachers had been schooled by the Brethren of the Common Life (3:170).

The curriculum at Liége was typical of the schools of the Brethren of the Common Life. It was graded by year, a most practical innovation, and each year it had a specified program of study; that, too, was most practical. Boyd describes the program as including

> The rudiments of grammar in the *first* year, an easy book of selections in the *second*, a simple prose author and Latin prose in the *third*, historical writers and the first stages of Greek in the *fourth*, more advanced Greek, logic and rhetoric and original prose in the *fifth*, Greek literature and composition and more advanced logic and rhetoric in the *sixth*, Euclid and Roman Law, Aristotle and Plato in the *seventh*, and finally theology and disputations in the eighth (4:172).

As did all later schools on the Continent, in the British Isles, and in North America, Sturm's gymnasium accepted the plan of a graded school, as the schools of the Brethren had demonstrated it. When Horace Mann of Massachusetts and Henry Barnard of Connecticut, in the middle nineteenth century, visited the Continent and reported to their state school boards on the benefit of the graded school, the schools they commended were heirs to the organizational genius of the Brethren of the Common Life and to Sturm. Sturm's *Book on the Right Method of Founding Schools for Literary Education* (*De literarum ludies recte aperiendis liber*) of 1537 and *Class Letters* of 1565, written for the guidance of the teachers in his school, were used by European teachers and directors of schools for at least two centuries.

Sturm opened his gymnasium in Strassburg in 1537; the publication of his *Book on the Right Method of Founding Schools for Literary Education* really advertised what his school intended to accomplish and how. Perhaps Sturm had in mind Isocrates, whose major treatise on education in fact advertised the objectives of his new school. But Sturm was no Isocrates, who would have been dismayed to learn that an influential

61

school had as its objective the acquisition by the students of a "pure, eloquent Ciceronian Latin." This was the very "rhetorical sophism" that Plato had rebuked and that Isocrates and Cicero, as well as Quintilian, denied to be the purpose of studying oratory and rhetoric. How strange it would have been for those great rhetoricians to see Sturm rejecting teaching which aimed at the hope of preparing informed and thoughtful citizens. Ciceronianism had claimed Sturm, who wrote that "men have a nature more ready for speech than for thought and judgment. . . ." (4:196) "Knowledge and purity and elegance of diction, should become the aim of scholarship, and towards its attainment both teachers and pupils should seduously bend their every effort." The personality of the director was so strong, and the organization of his gymnasium so impressive, that Sturm's way captured the academic secondary school of Continental Europe.

Sturm was not obsessed by some private philosophy of education. Where had he become infatuated with the ideal of Latin eloquence as an end of education in an age which had found its way to great advances in science and technology? This was, after all, the period of Galileo, Kepler, Newton, Descartes, and Leibniz. Sturm had gone to a university in Louvain, the Trilingual College founded by Erasmus. Though Erasmus condemned the Ciceronian "cult of imitation," his books on education all were designed to improve instruction in Latin composition and rhetoric. But Sturm was far less vigorous than his master, Erasmus, in sticking to the intention that Latin grammar and rhetoric lead to an improved quality of living. Like Isocrates, Erasmus held that "culture had its justification in the fact that it bears directly on good living." Erasmus succeeded in carrying this practical philosophy of education to England, where he was a major influence in the thinking of educators. Sturm's satisfaction with mastering Ciceronian eloquence, however, was a more potent force in directing the education of the European mainland.

WHEN HUMANISM WAS
COURTLY AND WORLDLY

There was but a passing revival during the seventeenth or eighteenth centuries of the Promethean humanism Aeschylus had urged so movingly in *Prometheus Bound*. But a fine, rather than a mean or grasping worldliness did appear to afford educators a path different from that pointed out by Sturm and the Ciceronians. Although this worldly humanism evolved a literature much superior to that of Sturm and other Ciceronians, once again it lacked the persuasive force that would have existed had its schools given the educational world concrete examples of theory being carried out in practice. The schools were not at hand, however. For six years Milton was a headmaster in England, but there is hardly a record of the accomplishment of his school or of its effects.

The reason why the ideas of worldly humanism never moved out of essays into practice was that *their proponents were indifferent to mass education*. They were tutors to royalty and nobility, and this singularly narrow focus on aristocratic leadership, with its consequent narrowness of definition as to who might become excellent, condemned worldly humanism, *then and now*, to near-ineffectuality, however splendid its literature.

The worldly humanist was not simply a variant of the conservative tradition of Greece, so well-described in Havelock's *Liberal Tradition in Greek Politics*. Though those they tutored were aristocrats, they did not write to defend a conservative position in political theory. Although Rousseau's imaginary tutee Émile was the heir of an aristocrat, Rousseau himself took a place in the forefront of the radical, revolutionary democratic movement of the eighteenth century. Likewise John Locke, with his view that the sovereign had no divine right to govern, but governed under a contract with the people, was not a defender of the conservative tradition.

The leadership that the worldly humanists sought to educate was, of course, secular rather than religious. The story of their undertaking in the education of the aristocracy runs back to the unsuccessful bid of Cassiodorus (*c.* 490-585) to school the young Gothic king, Athalaric, in the face of opposition from the Gothic nobles in Rome, who insisted that a ruler had no need for a literary education. Although Alcuin made headway with Charlemagne in the eighth century, the instruction of the Carolingian court was pathetically rudimentary. Nor was the literary education of the chivalrous knight one that would have impressed any humanist of the Renaissance. Nevertheless, the students of Cassiodorus, Alcuin, or any instructor in a feudal manor or castle were the same as those later taught by Vittorino, such as Frederigo, later Duke of Urbino. Frederigo had been an apt and favorite pupil of Vittorino, and his court later reflected his education. So polished was it, for all its worldly pleasures, that it became the setting for the foremost book of worldly humanism, the *Book of the Courtier* (*Il Cortegiano*), published in 1528 by Baldassare Castiglione (1478-1529). One notes that Castiglione's title was in Italian. The worldly humanists tended to be nationalistic, less men of all humanity than was Erasmus. Castiglione lived out the responsibility of the educator and counselor of princes. When Rome fell to the Spaniards under Charles V, Castiglione was discredited for his share in failing to avert the tragedy. But he had showed himself a man who practiced the leadership for which he prepared others.

After Castiglione, there was to be a succession of worldly, courtly humanists flourishing in Italy during the fifteenth and sixteenth centuries. "No single word," Baldwin insists, "is more characteristic of Renaissance literature than *courtier*" (2:12). The merchant princes were no less eager to have their humanists than were the landowning princes. In Venice, Minturno addresses the preface of his *De poeta* to Gabriel Vinea, "pride of commerce, delight of scholars" (2:13). In France, Guillaume Budé (1468-1540) endowed French with the phrase *le galant homme* in his *On the Education of the Prince*, written for young King Francis of France. The gallant Budé was a perfect courtier as pictured by Castiglione.

But it was in England that worldly humanism did best, managing to leave a strong impression on English education, especially on English private boys' schools, the so-called "great public schools." In these schools, which never lost their monopoly of prestige in English education, there was a genuine merger of Christian and worldly humanism. Also in England, Sir Thomas Elyot (1490-1546) published his *The Boke Named the Governour*. Elyot had been a student of Thomas Linacre, a scholarly physician who was said to have brought the Renaissance to England. Linacre, Sir Thomas More, Colet, Dean of St. Paul's Cathedral (and the one charged with revitalizing its cathedral school), and their Dutch friend Erasmus constituted the most active humanist group in Europe during the sixteenth century. Their common interest was in classic literature and in its merits for the education of young aristocrats, the future governors of England. The curriculum they would have set met the standards of any educated Athenian, even down to the place afforded sports and games.

The aristocratic narrowness of the worldly humanists did not handicap the Christian humanists, to whom history owes the first clear statements on the need for everyone to be literate (although they at no time assumed that all should have a secondary or grammar school education, which for all humanists would consist of the difficult and impractical substance of classic languages and literature). No worldly humanist would have outlined such a plan of mass education as did John Knox (1505-1572), spiritual leader of the early Scottish Calvinist Church, in his *First Book of Discipline*, which he prepared with four other ministers as a plan of education under Church control "for all classes of the community, which for breadth and comprehensiveness has no peer among the educational proposals of this period" (4:201). His scheme called for the establishment of universities, "great Schollis" to which both the youth of the rich and the poor were to come, the latter supported by the Church.

> . . . till tryell be tackin, whethir the spirit of docilitie be fund in them or not. Yf thei be fund apt to letteris and learnyng then may thei not (me meane, neathir the sonis of the riche, nor yit the sonis of the poore) be permittit to reject learnyng; but most be chareit to coinew thair studie, sa that the Commonwealthe may have some comfort by them (4:202).

The Christian humanists were not democrats, in the sense that worldly humanists like Rousseau and Locke were democrats; they were concerned with the immortal fate of all souls. They were committed to fight on the side of the hosts of the Lord against the hosts of the Fallen Angel. Mindful of that titanic and perpetual struggle, Luther spoke to those who governed the German towns and cities.

> If the magistrates may compel their able-bodied subjects to carry a pike and musket and do military service, there is much more reason for them compelling their subjects to send their children to school. For there is a far worse war to be waged with the devil, who employs himself secretly in injuring towns and States through the neglect of education (4:189).

With an eye to this same timeless warfare between the powers of Light and Darkness, the Puritan General Court of the Massachusetts Bay Colony in Colonial America in 1647 ruled to put teeth into an earlier order of 1642, both orders promulgated to confound "that Old Deluder Satan." The order of 1642 called on parents and masters with apprentices to see to it that their young charges could and did read the Scriptures and catechisms. In 1647, compliance being unsatisfactory, fines were ordained for delinquency, and every town of fifty or more families were to *appoint and support* locally a teacher of reading and writing; in every town of 100 families a schoolmaster was to be appointed to give instruction in Latin grammar. The Old Deluder could not be fought unless there was a learned (in the grammar and literature of the "holy languages") ministry to lead the assault.

In October, 1636, the General Court of the Massachusetts Bay Colony voted money "towards a schoale or colledge," and by 1642 the first class of nine members was graduated from Harvard College. In the following year, a twenty-six-page tract was published in London: *New England's First Fruits*. This described the natural resources, the climate, opportunities for converting the heathen, and made a special point of describing the thriving young college (15:700). The sentence describing the establishment of Harvard College is one of the most revealing testimonies to the Puritan desire that its leadership be tutored.

65

> After God had carried us safe to New England, and wee had builded our houses, provided necessaries for our liveli-hood, rear'd convenient places for Gods worship, and setled the Civil Government: One of the next things we longed for, and looked after was to advance *Learning* and perpetuate it to Posterity; dreading to leave an illiterate Ministery to the Churches, when our present Ministers shall lie in the Dust (15:701).

JOHN MILTON,
THE SUMMATION OF CHRISTIAN
AND WORLDLY HUMANISM

Though Milton (1608-1674) wrote very little on education, while John Locke (1632-1704) wrote much more, Milton's career reflects the more harmonious blend of Christian and worldly humanism. There is next to nothing in Locke's long *Some Thoughts Concerning Education* (1693) that were not to be read in Quintilian's *Institutes of Oratory*, not that Locke was not a most intelligent representative of that same happy confluence of Christian and worldly humanism. Locke was worldly—a good student of science and of psychology (see his *Essay Concerning Human Understanding*, 1690), as well as personal secretary to his friend, the powerful Earl of Shaftesbury. He was also Christian in his thoughts on education, though admittedly religion plays a rather minor role in the make-up of Locke's ideal man, possessed of a sound and exercised body, virtue, wisdom, good breeding, and learning. This had been said before, though Locke may have been a bit more frank about lowering the place of learning as opposed to good breeding, sound character, and an exercised body. He slid off a little in the direction of heartiness, away from the sophistication of the other humanists.

Milton moved to an independent position in religion, but retained many of the attributes of Puritanism, writing that the purpose of education ". . . is to repair the ruins of our first parents by requiring to know God aright, and out of that knowledge to love him, to imitate him, to be like him, as we may the nearest by possessing our souls of true virtue, which being united to the heavenly grace of faith makes up the highest perfection" (6:4). The best known of Milton's poems, *Paradise Lost* (1667), was both a religious testament and a testimony to the author's command of classic Greek and Roman literature. Milton freighted the poem with such a weight of classical allusion that today it would be criticized as a parade of learning. In its own day the display was fitting.

In part, the very fact that Milton could write poetry was a sign of worldliness. Was not the courtier, the knight, able to wax poetic? But Milton offered more evidence of worldly occupation. He was Latin secretary to Oliver Cromwell while Cromwell governed the British Commonwealth from 1649-1655. Latin still was the language of diplomacy, of international relations, and in his role as Latin secretary Milton felt called upon to play the part of an Isocrates, to "counsel and admonish the state" (6:30). The counsel and admonition was not to be administered through spoken but written orations. Milton consciously followed Isocrates ". . . who from his private house," Milton remembered, "wrote that discourse to the Parliament of Athens." The discourse which Milton assumed would be known to his educated readers was the plea of Isocrates that Athens take the lead in uniting the Greek city-states and leading them against the Persians.

Turning to Milton's thoughts concerning education, one finds him typical of those who opposed the Ciceronians and the forced-feeding of Latin and Greek grammar. Milton's *Tractate on Education* (1644) sneeringly refers to what passed for classical studies as "that asinine feast of sowthistles and brambles . . . words, words, words." The *Tractate* appeared seven years after Milton began to head his own grammar school, or academy, as it was called. His experience had convinced him that the right path of learning was "laborious indeed at the first ascent," becomes "so smooth, so green, so full of goodly prospect, and melodious sounds on every side, that the harp of Orpheus was not more charming" (6:9).

To follow this path, Milton, as Locke, had to find a means of paring down the Ciceronian diet of Latin and Greek. Milton was clear. "First," he wrote, "we do amiss to spend seven or eight years merely in scraping together so much miserable Latin and Greek, as might be learnt otherwise easily and delightfully in one year" (6:5). To make the study "delightful," Milton mounted the highroad that was to lead to Rousseau, Ben Franklin, and those educators of the eighteenth and nineteenth centuries who insisted that students pursue studies in terms of their applicability to the world. Milton would have his students read Latin works on agriculture so that they might learn ". . . hereafter to improve the tillage of their country, to recover the bad soil, and to remedy the waste that is made of good: for this was one of Hercules' praises" (6:13). In pointing to study for the improvement of man's lot, Milton added Promethean humanism to his Christian and worldly humanism. This was the philosophy of Francis Bacon (1561-1626), who had become the spokesman in England for the Promethean viewpoint that service to mankind is noble. In following Bacon, Milton inevitably was led to make room in the curriculum for the natural science that Bacon had pronounced to be the chief servant of man. But the day for the Protheans had not yet arrived.

Milton would have students pass through the *quadrivium* with geography substituted for music. They would study geometry, mathematics (arithmetic), astronomy, and geography, and then pass to "the instrumental sciences of Trigonometry and from thence to Fortification, Architecture, Enginry, or Navigation. And in Natural Philosophy they may proceed leisurely from the history of meteors, minerals, plants and living creatures as far as Anatomy."

> And now lastly will be the time to read with them those organic arts which enable men to discourse and write perspicuously, elegantly, and according to the fitted style, of lofty, mean, or lowly. Logic therefore so much as is useful, is to be referred to this due place with all her well couched heads and topics, until it be time to open her contracted palm into a graceful and ornate Rhetoric . . . to which Poetry would be made subsequent, or indeed rather precedent, as being less subtle and fine, but more simple, sensuous and passionate. From hence and not till now will be the right season of forming them to be able writers and composers in every excellent matter, when they shall be fraught with an universal insight into things (6:18-19).

"As near as I can guess, by reading," Clark writes in conclusion to his study of Milton's views on education,

Milton's school would be more like that of Isocrates than like the others, for only Isocrates oriented his school towards preparing his pupils "to Speak in Parliament or Council," by making all liberal knowledge function through rhetoric, or more accurately, through that "philosophy of the logos" which included all the arts of communication in language: grammar, rhetoric, and logic. Based as it was on similar assumptions Milton's own school of St. Paul's was well calculated to breed up her favored son as the renowned Orator, Historian, and Poet that he became (6:252).

In locating something of a revival of Promethean humanism in the seventeenth century, one risks seeming to make a spurt of interest in natural science equivalent to a Promethean mood. We have been at some pains to point out that interest in natural science had been quick to take hold in the later Middle Ages. England had had Robert Grosseteste and Roger Bacon long before it had the advertising of natural science written by Francis Bacon. The new Promethean element in the later Middle Ages was the belief that the pursuit of the natural sciences would advance the progress of man intellectually and materially. The idea of progress and of service to mankind is all-important.

68

Splendid as this revival of Promethean humanism was in spirit, its proponents indulged in a good deal of unseemly hatcheting of the opposition. Satire was their weapon. As Erasmus had used it in *In Praise of Folly* to damn the Ciceronians, so Rabelais (1494-1553) used in *Gargantua and Pantagruel*. Rabelais, priest and physician, hoped to replace what he thought to be medieval pedantry with a study of natural science, the *new* science, as formulated by the great Greek natural scientists who wrote on physics, mathematics, medicine, and zoology. Rabelais was one of the most appreciative of what Greek science had been (3:108). Medievalism, Scholasticism, and Ciceronianism were made one target by Rabelais, and those who did not know and appreciate the genuine intellectual interests of the medieval scholars were vastly amused and ready to bury the past, the "scholastic grossness of barbarous ages," as even Milton, betrayed by prejudice, was to describe them.

Both Gargantua and Pantagruel were described by Rabelais, as giants, performing Herculean feats both of stupidity and of greatness. The early education of Gargantua was the very epitome of all the nonsense of which Rabelais was certain medieval educators had been capable. Holofernes, "a great sophist and Doctor of Theology," taught the young king and giant

his A, B, C's so well, that he could say it by heart backwards; and this took him five years and three months. Then he read to him *Donat, le Facet, Theodolet,* and *Alanus in Parabolis*. These took him thirteen years, six months and two weeks. But you must remember that in the meantime he did learn to write in Gothic characters, and that he wrote all his books; for the art of printing was not then in use. . . . After that was read unto him *De Modis Significandi* and . . . a rabble of others; and herein he spent more than eighteen years and eleven months, and was so well versed therein that in school disputes with his fellow-students, he would recite it by heart backwards; and he did sometimes prove on his fingers' ends to his mother that *De Modis Significandi* was not scientific. Then was read to him the *Compost* on which he spent sixteen years and two months. And at that very time, his preceptor died of the pox (19:I, 43).

One important cause for the cruel representations of the Middle Ages made by most Renaissance intellectuals was printing. When movable type was introduced to Europe at the close of the fifteenth century, there was a great demand for books (2:37), and authors inundated printers with manuscripts. The new presses published both the classical antiquities and the writings of contemporary authors. There was little demand for treatises written (most of them commentaries on Christian writers, Aristotle, and critics of Aristotle) during the Middle Ages. These were held to be old hat. Thus ". . . the early printers helped to cut off their contemporaries and their successors from the immediately preceding centuries" (3:37-38).

Unhappily, the Renaissance appraisal of the Middle Ages was underwritten also by the Protestant leaders, notably by Calvin, who found the Middle Ages a period of corrupted faith (*medium saeculum*). Luther and Calvin did not follow their condemnation of the Middle Ages with any endorsement of the "new science" and "new philosophy." Luther was superstitious and especially opposed to astronomy (3:54). Calvin was heartily opposed to scientific inquiry: "He had no patience with idle curiosity, not much with scientific curiosity" (3:54). Nor was Calvin any less suspicious of the new science and new philosophy. "He was against the new astronomy, and if his common sense sometimes asserted itself against astrology and palmistry, he was none the less superstitious. He believed in witchcraft, as everyone else did, but his mind ran far more than many men's on fearful tales of ghosts and the devil" (3:46).

To most men, however, the new science and the new philosophy were irresistible. Men could make use of discoveries; indeed, they desired invention. The favor the English kings showed the Royal Society of London, founded in 1662, was positive proof of the prestige enjoyed by scientific inquiry at the close of the seventeenth century. Although most scientists would have agreed with the Royal Society's secretary, Edmund Halley, that science should study "the uses and properties of . . . things for helping mankind" (4:117), pure as well as applied science gained in strength and were given every approval. For the future of education, the happy light in which technology or applied science was seen portended the later respect for applied studies and perhaps, in the long run, even for vocational education.

1. ATKINS, J. W. H., *English Literary Criticism: The Medieval Phase.* New York: Cambridge University Press, 1943.

2. BALDWIN, CHARLES S., *Renaissance Literary Theory and Practice;* Donald L. Clark, ed. New York: Columbia University Press, 1939.

3. BARKER, ERNEST, GEORGE CLARK, and P. VAUCHER, eds., *The European Inheritance,* Vol. II. Oxford: The Clarendon Press, 1954.

4. BOYD, WILLIAM, *The History of Western Education.* London: A. & C. Black, 1952.

5. BUTTS, R. FREEMAN and LAWRENCE A. CREMIN, *A History of Education in American Culture.* New York: Holt, Rinehart & Winston, Inc., 1953.

6. CLARK, DONALD L., *John Milton at St. Paul's School.* New York: Columbia University Press, 1948.

7. COMENIUS, JOHN AMOS, *Orbis pictus,* tr. by Charles Hoole. Syracuse, N. Y.: C. W. Bardeen, Publisher, 1887.

8. DRAKE, WILLIAM E., *The American School in Transition.* Englewood Cliffs, N. J.: Prentice-Hall, Inc., 1955.

9. FLEMING, SANFORD, *Children and Puritanism.* New Haven: Yale University Press, 1933.

10. FORD, PAUL L., ed., *The New England Primer.* New York: Dodd, Mead & Co., 1899.

11. GRAVES, FRANK P., *Peter Ramus and the Educational Reformation of the Sixteenth Century.* New York: The Macmillan Co., 1912.

12. HUGHES, THOMAS, *Loyola.* New York: Charles Scribner's Sons, 1902.

13. KATINGS, N. W., *The Great Didactic of John Amos Comenius.* London: A. & C. Black, 1910.

14. MEYER, ADOLPHE E., *An Educational History of the American People.* New York: McGraw-Hill Book Co., Inc., 1957.

15. MILLER, PERRY and THOMAS H. JOHNSON, *The Puritans.* New York: American Book Company, 1938.

16. MONTAIGNE, MICHAEL, *The Essayes,* Vol. I, tr. by John Florio. London: Oxford University Press, 1924.

17. MORRIS, EDWARD E., ed., *Milton, Tractate of Education.* London: Macmillan & Co., Ltd., 1895.

18. NELSON, JOEL S., *Aeneae Silvii de liberorum educatione.* Washington, D.C.: The Catholic University of America Press, 1940.

19. RABELAIS, FRANÇOIS, *Gargantua and Pantagruel,* Vol. I, tr. by Jacques Le Clercq. New York: The Heritage Press, 1942.

20. SMALL, WALTER H., *Early New England Schools.* Boston: Ginn & Company, 1914.

21. WOOD, NORMAN, *The Reformation and English Education.* London: Routledge & Kegan Paul, Ltd., 1931.

22. WOODWARD, WILLIAM H., *Desiderius Erasmus.* New York: Cambridge University Press, 1904.

23. ———, *Vittorino Da Feltre and Other Humanist Educators.* New York: Cambridge University Press, 1921.

70

The enlargement of educational opportunity has meant more than merely the greater access to schooling by a larger proportion of the population. Educational opportunity has also been understood as the expanding of the course of study to include such subjects as vocational offerings, scarcely found in schools prior to the eighteenth century.

Since the eighteenth century, educational opportunity in both of these senses has been fought for by reformers whose dedication has been rewarded with many more victories than defeats. The growing economies of many Western nations abetted this extension of educational opportunity. As a result, all countries with advanced economies now have fully developed programs of elementary education, available to all children, as well as plans for a comprehensive system of secondary schooling that will serve most adolescents.

Schooling on such a large scale did not exist in the eighteenth century. Where it did, as in secondary schooling for example, it was not conceived of as education for all youth. The humanistic secondary school was

71

NATIONALISM, WEALTH, AND EDUCATIONAL OPPORTUNITY

6

for the sons and occasionally for the daughters of the upper class. Those who were to be groomed to be the leaders of society, the elite, were educated. The gradual entry into schools of a large number of children from homes that were not aristocratic is the prime historical fact of modern education. Nor can this fact be separated from its mate, the addition of subjects of study that would not have been thought of as education in earlier times. Vocational subjects especially would have been repugnant to the men of ancient Greece, and to their intellectual descendants.

Would children and youth, some destined by their social background to be leaders in the professions and in business, ever attend school with those from the lower social strata, destined to become workers, or, if they were lucky, to have vocational training? In the United States, an affirmative answer could have been expected in the nineteenth century. In Europe, the winning of a single school system for children of all social classes erupted into a classic battle, fought for forty years following the Armistice of 1918. Closely tied with that battle for a single, comprehensive school system, aimed at reducing the social distance between classes, was one intended to gain "parity of esteem," a British phrase, between humanistic, scientific, and vocational studies.

These changes in education were articulated by reformers who urged the merits of democratic liberty and a Republican form of government, in which individual citizens would be responsible for intelligent civic action. It did not take long to recognize that democracy and Republican government depended on the schooling of men.

Perhaps one of the major oversights in writing the record of the extension of educational opportunity in modern times has been the neglect of the earnest pursuit of that opportunity by religious groups, Catholic, Protestant, and Jewish. It may be that one of the revisions of perspective on the history of education, both in the United States and abroad, will be to provide more adequate recognition for the commitment of religious congregations to schools, both parochial and public. In part, no doubt, that commitment was part of an anxiety that without education faith would slip away. But just as real was the belief in education engendered by a moral position that considered it essential that individuals be able to develop their characters. As in the seventeenth century, religious leaders of the nineteenth knew that character development was most unlikely without schooling.

Powerful as allies of enlargement of educational opportunity were the elements of the burgeoning economy in the eighteenth, nineteenth, and twentieth centuries. Capitalism, supported in northern countries and in the United States by the "Protestant Ethic," preaching thrift and productivity, and teamed with the mechanical-industrial revolution made possible by science, called for more schooling, furnishing both the practical reason and the money for its support.

Far from negligible as an influence in the expansion of education was the fact that rulers realized that in an educated population there is strength. When the chief of state was a king with great power, the benefits he customarily sought were productive and loyal subjects, but his wishes ordinarily were also behind the extension of educational opportunity, though to a notably more modest degree than the Republican urgings of a Thomas Jefferson or a liberal like Condorcet (14).

"THE WEALTH OF NATIONS
AND THE POWER OF STATES"

The title of this section comes from a chapter heading in the second volume of *The European Inheritance* (2). What better phrase to describe the two most potent forces to combine to foster a great expansion in state-supported, public education within which, because of the economic interests at work, practical or vocational studies would gain at least a minor place? The enlightened despotism which existed in most of the nations of mid-eighteenth century Europe gave rise to leaders who were very much inspired with national pride and ambition, leaders who had a centralized authority which could order into existence a system of universal, compulsory primary education. A bureaucracy to enforce and execute it would be a natural offspring of the order. After this fashion *national* systems of education were born. In nations without kings, hereditary aristocracy, or established church, the benefits of mass education had to be preached, as they were in the American colonies and later in the United States by many, though rarely as eloquently as by Thomas Jefferson.

Nevertheless, neither decrees of kings, act of Congress, nor letters and speeches of reformers had a thrust as powerful as that of economic and social changes. Without these changes, reformers would not have been able to carry their point, nor would the minimal standards of educational opportunity commanded by the kings have been much increased had not leaders of finance, business, industry, and labor sensed the utility of more and more varied education. These economic changes are usually associated with capitalism and something called dramatically the industrial revolution. Together, industrialism and capitalism made the growth of cities certain. They produced masses of urban workers, a poor, wretched proletariat, who became the objects of intense pity of such reformers as Charles Dickens.

Science was no less a factor in these economic changes; indeed, science made the "mechanical revolution," perhaps a more accurate phrase, possible. Without progress in the physical sciences and mathematics, it is most unlikely that there would have been the invention of machines, without which certainly there could have been no factories, no industrial revolution. But the invention of machines to multiply man's effort in spinning, weaving, mining, and transporting focus undue attention on the eighteenth century. Essential economic forces already had been set in play; beginning in the sixteenth century, for example, there was a constant improvement in transport (2:126).

Though there has been altogether too little attention on the history of the technological transformation of agriculture beginning in the late nineteenth century, manufacture leading up to it had begun its metamorphosis a century before. Between 1733 and 1779, British scientists and technicians recast the textile industry of their country, taking production from a handicraft stage to the threshold of full mechanization and industrialization. The "fly shuttle" was announced in 1773 by John Kay, one of the most important inventors contributing to the technology that remade the weaving industry before 1800.

Kay's early shuttle, his multiple shuttle boxes of 1760, the Jacquard spinning machine, Hargreaves' "spinning jenny" of 1764, and, finally, Edmund Cartwright's power loom of 1785—these inventions and others gave substance to the industrial revolution. After the machine doomed handicraft industry, specialization of work, increased production, urban pooling of labor, and modern industrialization and urbanism became possible, and with them increased demand for education.

RESPONSE OF EDUCATORS TO THE ECONOMIC AND SOCIAL CHANGES OF THE SEVENTEENTH, EIGHTEENTH, AND NINETEENTH CENTURIES

No one interested in education during the early industrial period could have been expected to have foreseen the opportunities to come, both for vocational training and for courses, as those in "industrial arts," that aimed to provide an understanding of fabrication in the modern industrial age. The original response to the changes being wrought was a response to horrifying social conditions. Referring to a period from 1776 to 1850, Clough and Cole, historians of European economic development, have instructed their readers on the unhappy circumstances of the urban workers who labored sixteen hours a day only to support themselves in squalor (8:513).

A poor man's life had a disheartening quality, whether he was a factory hand or a farmer. This was what caught the eye of many with humanitarian consciences, men and women who had been educated in a humanistic tradition in which they had learned to honor conditions that encouraged men to develop to the full measure of their human potentiality. The conditions that Hogarth depicted in his drawings, that Dickens made the environment of so many of his novels, fostered their share of educational plans. To the Swiss reformer Pestalozzi (1746-1827), education was the most promising means of insuring men the ability to be independent, an ability he and so many other reformers felt necessary in order for men to flourish as human beings.

Thus it was that from the seventeenth to the late nineteenth century, there were two educational messages abroad in the West. These joined almost as twins, but could have been identified separately. One was humanitarian, asking for help and charity for the children of the poor. This philanthropy, in part, was to take the form of teaching these orphans, juvenile delinquents, and pauper children such marketable skills as weaving or operating a simple lathe.

The twin of humanitarian response was more emphasis upon vocational education, not as an adjunct of philanthropy or as treatment of delinquents or orphans, but as proper training for young men and women who would have to go to work at the completion of elementary school, or certainly after high school graduation.

A third response certainly was made; it was typified by the early manual arts movement in the United States. Here could be found the claim, still very much alive, that education in manual arts or in industrial arts, the successor to manual arts, was sound general education. Advocates took their cue from the eighteenth century philosopher Rousseau (1712-1778), who maintained that experience with the planning and workmanship of carpentry or any other manual art disciplined mind, hand, and character.

FROM HUMANITARIAN RESPONSE
TO "EDUCATIONAL REALISM"
AND VOCATIONAL EDUCATION

Of the three voices that made themselves heard, the first raised was humanitarian. Conditions of the lower class were sufficiently miserable to command the attention of many who were not educators. There was sufficient pressure on governments in Europe (the United States lagged in providing social welfare legislation) to enact laws instructing local communities to feed, clothe, and shelter paupers and children of paupers. The latter were also to learn a trade. The Netherlands had such legislation by 1581. In 1601, the English Poor Law was passed. The schools that resulted from the Poor Law became the famous "charity schools," certainly commendable in themselves but destined to stigmatize elementary education in the nineteenth century as charity to be furnished by the state to children of parents too poor to pay for instruction. It would be many years before the stigma of "charity schooling" was lifted from free, public, elementary schooling in the United States and abroad.

Humanitarian educational reformers in Switzerland, England, and Germany led the humanitarian movement. As these men were religious, their philanthropy welled from Christian conscience. The movement in England was a case in point. As the factories of England multiplied, children as young as five years of age came to them as workers. The Sunday school, introduced by a Gloucester publisher, Robert Raikes, was devised to give these children some bit of schooling on the one day of the week when they would not be in the factory.

No one really knows who pioneered this philanthropy, but surely August Hermann Francke (1663-1727) was among the first (13:244-254). Francke exemplified the religious conscience behind the early philanthropic extension of educational opportunity. It was German *pietism*, an evangelical Protestantism, that fired Francke. Believing that to honor God with truly Christian behavior was the supreme end of life, he undertook to collect funds with which to teach poor children to read and sing in order to make them to be active in the church services, where the voices of children led the congregation in song.

The poor children of Glauchau, Germany, who came to Francke, learned more than the rudiments of reading, singing, and Scripture. Spinning, sewing, and knitting also were taught, but not as skills with which later to earn a living. The little ragamuffins who took shelter with Francke wore shreds and patches, and they were taught what they needed to know in order to clothe themselves. If they were receiving vocational training, that was incidental; it would have been too much to expect of Francke, who was both a minister in Glauchau and a professor of oriental languages and Protestant theology.

Perhaps the more interesting venture in education in which Francke embarked was his *Pädagogium*, a school for young aristocrats where a classical humanistic course of study (from which Hebrew was not absent) was conjoined with modern, "realist" studies—German, French, mathematics, physics, mineralogy, astronomy, botany, anatomy, geography, history, painting, and music. However superficially some of these were treated, the breadth of the course of study in Francke's Pädagogium won his school universal attention in Europe. Indeed, the Pädagogium was the direct forebear of the modern European academic secondary schools. Two centuries after Francke's death, it had evolved into three separate secondary courses of study in Europe, one concentrating on Greek, Latin, and modern foreign languages, a second specializing in modern foreign languages, but finding a place for Latin and some history and science, and the third looking to science for the core of its concentration, though not neglecting modern foreign languages.

Johann Julius Hecker (1707-1768) and the Realschule. Teachers have been best-known by the needs of their students. In Hecker's case, the student stands in contrast with the teacher. Johann Julius Hecker (13:254-256) sat at Francke's feet at the University of Halle, and after graduating taught in the Pädagogium. Hecker, too, was a pietist and a pastor. In 1739, he succeeded to the pastorate of Trinity Church, Berlin, and, as Francke, opened a school.

Francke had been dead for twenty years when his pupil announced the *Oekonomisch–Mathematische Realschule.* It was a trade school, started with the approving interest of the Prussian king. The Realschule had caught the fancy of the king because it seemed to promise a type of education that would prepare men to be productive. The differences between the Realschule and the Latin school or Pädagogium of Francke were manifest. The latter left glass blowing as an extracurricular activity, whereas Hecker took a step toward vocational training and put classes in glass blowing, agriculture, bookkeeping, and mining at the heart of the course of study. The elements of physics, chemistry, geometry, mechanics, architecture, drawing, botany, and mineralogy were in the course of study too, but Hecker frankly avowed his Realschule to be vocational.

What Hecker did was to create a school which really set out to instruct in work with which its graduates would make their living. Hecker did not intend the course of study of the Realschule to provide a good, general education. He did not pretend that these courses employed the very best methods of teaching arithmetic or reading, for example. That was left to Rousseau to say. For Hecker it was enough that the graduates of his school were favorably noticed far and wide. The king so thoroughly appreciated the practicality of Hecker's educational plans that he charged Hecker with drafting the Prussian school law of 1763, which made primary grade education compulsory and a charge on the public treasuries. To this day, the Realschules of Germany and of the Scandinavian countries are witnesses to Hecker's influence.

Rousseau and "Realism." The Swiss philosopher-educator Jean Jacques Rousseau (1712-1778), was a contemporary of Hecker; his life span overlapped that of Francke. His philosophy of education contained strains suggestive of both Francke and Hecker. Rousseau brought into the curriculum the manual arts, which Francke treated as peripheral. He did so without making schooling purely vocational, and he carefully avoided planning humanistic education for aristocratic children, reserving training of the hand for the offspring of the poor. The plan for education that Rousseau drew up was for all children. The instruction of Émile, the hero of Rousseau's major book on education, *Émile* (1762), really was meant to apply to children of paupers, burghers, and nobles alike. At its core were two ideas, one of which was humanitarian. Education in science and in mechanical and agricultural arts was the best help a poor boy could have. Inclining toward Hecker, Rousseau thought that instruction in mechanical and agricultural arts would help the student to earn his bread if that were necessary; if it were not, the student would have had an opportunity to learn all that a school need teach.

Rousseau based the latter conviction on his belief that the only reliable information that men had came from careful observation. In the history of thought, Rousseau's belief came to be termed empiricism. Rousseau was a keen observer himself; the knowledge that the carpenter had from observing and working at his trade struck Rousseau as reliable, for he had been a carpenter. In his youth, Rousseau had tried his hand in more than one apprenticeship; craftsmen were respected people in his eyes. Rousseau went further and made claims for manual training that were echoed again and again in the years that followed his death. For him, mechanical and agricultural crafts were superior to language and literature for *training the mind*. Writing on the history of manual and industrial education, Charles A. Bennett refers to Rousseau's thought that manual arts could be a means of mental training as marking "the beginning of a new era in education" (3:81).

Johann Heinrich Pestalozzi (1746-1827) and "Realism." Pestalozzi was one of those great men who are able to absorb the ideas of others without sacrifice of their own imagination. He was born in Calvinist Switzerland but, apparently, not an iota of the Calvinist thought concerning the sinful nature of man and his natural instincts remained with him. Experience taught Pestalozzi how harsh the life of the peasant was, but it did not make him a fatalist. He was the reformer par excellence.

Pestalozzi was an enormously enthusiastic reader of Rousseau, convinced like Rousseau that youth could learn essential academic skills while learning such practical arts as farming. Because he had to finance his schools with the produce grown on his farm, he endeavored to show that children of the poor could learn—could cultivate their intellectual and moral natures —through the same activities as earned their bread and made their clothes. As Rousseau, Pestalozzi saw no contradiction between manual activities and knowledge. To his home, Neuhof, located in Aargau, Switzerland, Pestalozzi brought twenty waifs who worked as they learned, but for all their work, they could not produce enough to sustain the farm, which went bankrupt too soon for anyone to be able to evaluate the effort of combining learning the three R's with learning to farm, spin yarn, weave, and to perform other practical arts.

When Neuhof failed, Pestalozzi took charge of the orphanage at Stanz, Switzerland, where he continued to try further Rousseau's theories. Again at Stanz, and later at Yverdun and Burgdorf, "things, work, and abstractions" were kept closely united. In 1782, he published the widely read novel *Leonard and Gertrude*, in which he had a first opportunity to tell a widely scattered audience of his humanitarian purposes. The book sketched a very moving picture of an impoverished home, kept together through the forebearance and work of the mother. Unhappily, readers seem to have been so gripped by the sentimental story that there was a minimum of discussion of the educational theory. The book's heroine, Gertrude, united handicrafts with the three R's in her successful efforts to keep her family together and to upgrade the poor of the village. Pestalozzi, who had no wish to write a best-seller, was disappointed with the favorable public reaction. He protested against the sentimental reaction to *Leonard and Gertrude* and wrote several rather dull tracts on the principles of education contained in the novel. Almost no one was interested in the tracts.

The disappointed Pestalozzi fell on hard times. There were periods of some prosperity, not for Pestalozzi and his family but for his ideas as reflected in the schools at Burgdorf and Yverdun. Between 1800 and 1804, Pestalozzi housed a boarding school for boys between the ages of six and eighteen in an old castle. When the town council ousted him in order to use the castle, he moved to Yverdun. There his school remained for twenty years, folding in 1825, two years before Pestalozzi's death. The only period in which Pestalozzi's ideas really flourished and attracted appreciative understanding was between 1805 and 1810. If one looked at what Pestalozzi preached and practiced in those good years his contribution became evident.

Above all, Pestalozzi had a commanding principle, a simple one indeed. Said he, every human being can be educated to attain a higher level of self-respect and power. *Pestalozzi riveted his attention on individuals.* No educator has been less intrigued with masses and the "mass man." Schooling was to proceed with increasing sensitivity to knowledge of how children grow and develop. Pestalozzi felt that by never turning aside from experiments using this knowledge of child growth and development, the schools would succeed to a greater and greater extent in helping individual children and youth help themselves.

If one were to ask whether Pestalozzi believed that there was a pattern of child development, of adolescent behavior and growth, the answer would have to be guarded. Pestalozzi shared the opinion of some eighteenth century philosophers that all things obeyed laws of orderly development. He seemed to feel quite sure that a child would unfold according to natural laws. To some extent, he wrote as though he knew these laws, but happily Pestalozzi was too little a philosopher to permit his theorizing on the order of nature to stand in the way of actually working with children and observing them.

In each of his schools, and sometimes there were as many as two hundred students enrolled, the atmosphere was not that of a school but of a home. The students were supported psychologically and encouraged. They had a place in the family, and their job was a family affair from which they learned about themselves, as well as about reading, writing, arithmetic, and other subjects. Doubtless, the most successful boarding schools of later times have functioned on principles best known to Pestalozzi.

The soundness of Pestalozzi's approach finally was recognized by men of power and wealth. The Tsar of Russia knighted him; France made him a "Citizen of the French Republic." The philosophers Fichte and Herbart knew and respected him. After 1808 the schools of Russia, always being organized and reorganized with an eye to superior practice, were redesigned to take account of Pestalozzi's ideas. The schools of Switzerland and teacher-training for those schools came under his influence. England and France sent students of education to observe Pestalozzi and his work at

Yverdun. The United States, too, was introduced to his ideas. In a way, Pestalozzi was the first European educator to make a major impression on American education after the Colonial period.

In a roundabout way, Edward S. Sheldon (1823-1897), superintendent of schools of Oswego, New York, chanced upon a display of materials for Pestalozzian "object lessons." Pestalozzi's standard practice was to associate anything being taught with an object or picture. It so happened that Sheldon saw them in Toronto, Canada, and learned that they were modeled after those used by the Home and Colonial Training College in London. This college, in turn, had been directed in its theory by Pestalozzi, or more accurately, by Dr. Charles Mayo and Dr. Elizabeth Mayo, who were experts in Pestalozzian materials and methods. Sheldon brought Miss M. E. M. Jones to Oswego from the Home and Colonial Training College for the express purpose of training teachers in the methods of Pestalozzi, especially the "sense realist" techniques of using objects in connection with teaching all abstractions, whether they were words, figures, or numbers. The students at the Oswego Normal School responded most enthusiastically to the Pestalozzian imports; each of them carried the word to the outside world after the fashion of enthusiastic reformers. Pestalozzi and sense realism were truly launched in America.

Philip Emanuel von Fallenberg (1771-1844) and Hofwyl. The most advantageous way for one to have met von Fallenberg in the history of education was to be introduced through Joseph Neff, director of a Parisian orphanage and school, both Pestalozzian in style. Neff was observed by a wealthy Philadelphian, Maclure, who persuaded Neff to leave Paris for Philadelphia, where he was given charge of a school in the city's suburbs. But Neff was a farmer and agriculturist, as was Pestalozzi. He moved the school into the country where he could practice according to the thesis held by Rousseau and Pestalozzi that youth should learn academic subjects in intimate connection with learning to farm. Village Green, where Neff opened his school, was too remote. Not even the children of farmers would come to school. A second venture in Louisville, Kentucky, also failed.

Neff failed but Pestalozzian ideas did not. They were rescued by a good friend of Pestalozzi, Philip Emanuel von Fallenberg. A philanthropist and humanitarian, von Fallenberg was devoted both to Pestalozzi and his theories. Von Fallenberg had the advantage of being wealthy and well-organized.

The link between Neff and von Fallenberg was provided by Neff's patron, Maclure, who was a frequent visitor to the schools of both Pestalozzi and von Fallenberg. There is no question that what Maclure really sought was a school where the students would work with tools and participate in activities that really taught them about the world in which they lived. Although Maclure had made a considerable fortune in urban business, it was too early to see the demands that industry and the city were making on life, and that a realistic education would have to be geared to these demands. Maclure was a restless man, wandering all over Europe in his quest for practical schooling; but he was not alone. On one of his trips he met another urban philanthropist and humanitarian, the celebrated Scotsman, Robert Owen. Maclure found that Owen shared his interests in education. Owen, too, had tried to underwrite a school for the poor in which they would learn self-respect through an increased power to understand, communicate, and produce.

Owen had invested substantial sums in the experiment, and had shown his sincerity by sending his two boys to the experimental school in Switzerland run by von Fallenberg. Owen and Maclure visited that school and then, together, embarked on a wholly new experiment, the organization of a whole colony in America, organized around educational principles straight from the writings of Comenius, Rousseau, and Pestalozzi. It was to be a socialistic experiment; the community was to be a utopia of the type dreamed of by men who felt that Man is basically sound, and can be nurtured to cooperate and develop nobly. New Harmony opened, it lived, and it failed.

Von Fallenberg, working on his farm in Hofwyl, Switzerland, did not try to create a socialistic utopia where men would not work for gain. Although the setting was rural and the spirit was cooperative, the drive of von Fallenberg was to make the students productive and independent, but not brutishly so. Von Fallenberg was a product of the Reformation, a deeply religious man, who thought of himself as his brother's keeper.

The farm school von Fallenberg used as a base for his operations was known far and wide. Von Fallenberg called it Hofwyl, and had selected it for many of the reasons that motivated da Feltre three centuries earlier. The farm was close by a town, but was hidden by hills and centrally located in rich farming land. Hofwyl actually housed not one, but three schools— one for the children of the lower classes (the Farm and Trade School), the Academy for upper-class students, and the School of Applied Science for the middle class.

The importance of these schools for education during the succeeding one hundred and fifty years was great. Charles Bennett, a historian of manual arts education, claimed that the Farm and Trade School became the model for both the agricultural reform schools and the industrial reform schools of the United States. More importantly, the idea of separate schools for each major social class was used later for all European schools. For the upper classes there were schools combining science and humanistic studies. For the middle class, the children of merchants, there were schools that prepared the future merchants. The purpose of the farm and trade schools for the lower classes is obvious. If one asked whether von Fallenberg honored the three schools equally, a most likely answer would be that he

81

considered all three schools excellent because they were suited to the needs of children of particular social classes which had little in common. The idea was Platonic and not inappropriate in a society where social classes were rigidly set apart and children lived their lives in the social class of their parents. However clearly von Fallenberg distinguished social classes, manual work was part of the curriculum in each school.

The middle-class boys in the School of Applied Science had opportunities for learning business practices which were truly unique for education of that time. These boys worked in the business office of the farm, where plans for planting, marketing, purchasing, and banking were made. In a way, the School of Applied Science had the widest curriculum. In it a boy could experience the courses of the Academy if he wished, and he was expected to take part in the labors of the farm, the shops, and, of course, the business office.

The business office was not the only link between the educational philosophy of Hofwyl and the new mechanical age of industry and agriculture. Von Fallenberg pursued one hobby more than any other, that of *scientific* agriculture. This involved the designing of farm machinery and its production in the Hofwyl shops. Students were expected to plan carefully the planting of crops, pasturage, and marketing. The school was more practical than its American rival, the Academy of Benjamin Franklin.

Benjamin Franklin's Academy. Benjamin Franklin (1706-1790) opened his Academy in Philadelphia in 1751. Its utilitarianism or realistic approach was premature; classical humanism was to dominate American education for at least another century. But Franklin was a venturesome man, much impressed by the moral to be found in Daniel Defoe's *Robinson Crusoe*. Crusoe had survived his perilous abandonment on a tropical isle because he combined genius with skills of hand that would have found high favor with Rousseau. Through *Robinson Crusoe*, Defoe preached the gospel of utilitarianism, to be made famous by the English philosopher, Herbert Spencer, in his essay, "What Knowledge Is of Most Worth," that appeared a century later. The philosophy of Franklin was utilitarian. This is not to say that he held religion or literary accomplishment in low esteem; he did not. Both moral and religious instruction had places in the course of study of the Academy. But he was outspoken against spending time with Latin, Greek, and Hebrew when there was so much English literature to be known, so much need for practice in English composition, and such great opportunities for those skilled in science and technology. It was from these studies that the curriculum of the Academy was made up. But the effort was premature, for no sooner had Franklin died than English was assigned a lesser place in the school; Latin was returned to the position of importance accorded it throughout the Western world in the eighteenth century. As though to emphasize the disdain the educational world had for Franklin's utilitarianism, the Academy which he saw as a school for preparing young people for useful work and citizenship became the model for the classical humanist, college-preparatory schools, first on the Atlantic seaboard, and then throughout the United States.

A PUBLIC HIGH SCHOOL

Franklin had been defeated, after his death, by the proponents of the view that only a classical humanist education was worthy of the name education. But because the needs of the modern world could not tolerate this definition of education, it was destined not only to be subverted but almost obliterated. The signs of the time were earliest visible in the United States when, in 1821, Boston opened an English Classical School. Within three years the word *classical* was dropped from the title, and before long even *English* disappeared. It was no longer necessary to advertise the fact that the vernacular language would dominate the curriculum!

In 1874, Justice Thomas M. Cooley of the Michigan Supreme Court rejected the claim of citizens in School District No. 1, Kalamazoo, asserting that the local Board of Education had no authority to collect and expend tax monies for the support of a public high school. "Having specifically provided for free elementary schools and a state university," Cooley concluded, "the state would be highly inconsistent if it forced parents to secure private secondary education" (6:419). Other states followed Michigan's lead and a complete system of public education was assured the United States before the end of the centuiy.

83

The United States Supreme Court's decision of 1925 in the case of *Pierce* v. *Society of Sisters* was to insure those who desired private schools for their offspring and were willing to finance the schooling freedom to patronize private schools.

Looking back over these key events, the development of general educational opportunity seems to have been gained with ease. This has not been the case, certainly not in the United States where the Constitution reserved responsibility for education to the several states. This reservation of the Tenth Amendment has been an important reason why public education in this country has been decentralized and under the control, largely, of state boards of education which have delegated a good deal of authority to local boards of education. In Europe and elsewhere, there have been both much more centralization in a national system of education and, necessarily, clearly visible authority over the education by professional educators.

In the United States it has been an uphill struggle for extension of educational opportunity, and prior to the emergence of the friends of the public schools, the fight was made locally by religious congregations and nationally by idealogues, chief among whom was Thomas Jefferson.

BIBLIOGRAPHY

See the references at the end of Chapter 7.

Thomas Jefferson (1743-1826) did not write about education in general, but thought of it specifically in terms of the needs of a republic. Above all, Jefferson was a republican, and after Cicero the next most articulate about what a republic is and what it demands for its sustenance. Like Cicero, Jefferson was a legislator, drafting legislation on education and on schools in and for a republic. On October 7, 1776, Jefferson entered the Virginia Assembly. Virginia had adopted a constitution, but had not formulated a code of laws or the machinery of government. To Jefferson fell the responsibility of drafting a series of bills comprehending a plan for a system of education in Virginia. This series of bills contained the core of what Jefferson felt to the best education for a republic.

Of course, Jefferson was not writing legislation for a national system of education. The republic was the sovereign, individual state. Alexander Hamilton, not Thomas Jefferson, advocated a strong central government, and had Hamilton written on

84

THE EXTENSION
OF EDUCATIONAL
OPPORTUNITY

7

education he might have gone on record in favor of a national system of schools. But Jefferson never deviated from his espousal of *decentralization*. In the matter of school control, he specifically stated that the control of schools should be lodged in the "ward"—an area some five or six miles square but smaller than a county. Jefferson proposed that the primary schools of wards too poor to support them be aided from county funds. Decentralization, localization of financial responsibility for, and control of, schools was the backbone of Jefferson's philosophy of educational organization and administration. It became the accepted pattern in this country, tying in well with the parish and township administrative organization that had emerged in the seventeenth and eighteenth centuries.

Jefferson authored three bills, submitting them between 1776 and 1779. They did not succeed in winning general approval in the Assembly, and were redrafted and submitted again in 1817. There is little difference between the bills of 1776-1779 and the legislation of 1817, however; the thinking on the earlier bills stood, though with modifications. Of the three offered, Jefferson favored the bill known as "A Bill for the More General Diffusion of Knowledge." This bill shows that Jefferson feared an ignorant populace; this fear was at the heart of his legislation on education. But how easily his fear was allayed! All the schooling that Jefferson felt it necessary to provide the children of Virginia to keep them from ignorance was three years at the primary level.

The "primaries," as Jefferson called them, were charged with instructing in the three R's. Reading, writing, and arithmetic were the only studies Jefferson felt that it was possible to guarantee everyone. The limit, however, was not set by monetary cost. Rather was it established on the thesis that most people are not educable beyond minimal literacy. It was left to later generations to find evidence for greater confidence in the learning capacity of the masses of people. The matter was clear in the mind of Jefferson: men could be divided into the small group of educable individuals and the far larger group of potential workers and shop keepers.

Equally clear in Jefferson's mind was the need for public financing of the schooling of any educable young man too poor to pay his way beyond the primaries. A practical man, Jefferson took pains to outline a plan for organizing the schools of Virginia in a way that he felt would provide for the worthy but indigent student. Each county of Virginia had its judge, and Jefferson suggested that the magistrate appoint a visitor to the primary school, among whose supervisory duties would be the selection of the brightest of the poor boys in the school. These lads were to be given scholarships to attend, free of any cost to them, one of the secondary or grammar schools of Virginia. Admission to the grammar schools was not to be limited to bright boys only; any other boy could come if his parents were able to afford his education. What Jefferson wished to insure was that any bright boy could get schooling at the expense of the state.

The precedent set by Jefferson was that free *public* schooling, beyond the primary level, should be available only to the bright; the less able were to be progressively weeded out. This point of view was first challenged effectively no earlier than in the 1940's, when students of education published their reasons for believing that there was a place in school for all students *if* the curriculum was modified to take account of individual differences.

The grammar school. Jefferson was a classical humanist who came to accept certain realistic modifications in the classical humanist curriculum. The grammar or secondary schools were to teach "the higher branches of numerical arithmetic," as Jefferson put it, together with Greek, Latin, and geography. This was his initial plan for the course of study. Later this initial listing was amended to include French, Spanish, Italian, and German (as electives), as well as English grammar, "mensuration" of land or surveying, the use of geographic globes, and the first principles of navigation.

Much more original was Jefferson's idea that Virginia should have a place in the secondary schools for poor but intellectually able boys. What he was proposing, in effect, was that Virginia demand of her citizens that they see to it that there be secondary schools. The tax burden for maintenance would not be great because the schools would charge fees. A degree of support and supervision of these grammar schools would come from a literary fund created by general taxation. As was to be expected, the scholarships for poor boys likewise would be borne by this fund.

The control of education. Jefferson has been thought of as a philosopher, and this would be a proper compliment if it did not detract from the appreciation of his organizational talents. The organization of public instruction in this country owes much to the models that Jefferson wrote into the legislation he helped to draft for Virginia. For example, Jefferson demonstrated that, if the principle of local control and support of schools established by the state were accepted, there would not be insuperable obstacles in the way of effecting suitable organizational structure. For the location of his grammar schools, Jefferson subdivided Virginia into nine districts. Each district was to have a *college*, a name Jefferson preferred for secondary schools, for in the English fashion they were to board students as well as instruct them. The construction and administration of these colleges Jefferson left to an independent board of public instruction.

The county judge was to appoint the visitors for the supervision of the primaries; the boards of public instruction for the supervision of the colleges were examples of a trend in the organization (and administration) of public education that emerged in the eighteenth century and came to be the classic form of school organization throughout the United States. Its essence and principle were simple. The state was to have ultimate authority in educational affairs, and the management of the schools was to be delegated to the counties and lesser geographical units, which were to see to the appointment of laymen personally responsible to the interests of the state and public. Today, our public and private schools have lay school boards which are the outgrowth of eighteenth century experiments in having the citizens oversee the work of the schools.

Jefferson's thoughts on the organization of the schools were typical of the eighteenth century's preference for decentralized organization and lay control. The only significant recent addition to this idea of decentralization has been a parallel to the development of professional management staffs in modern industry. Public and private schools have developed professional standards which have permitted the emergence of trained personnel. But the legal authority still resides where it was placed in the eighteenth century—in the state governments which provide the legal sanction and framework within which the lay boards consider policy.

The cost of schools. Jefferson rounded out his projection of what a republic needed in the way of schools by arguing the case for a state university. Like the secondary colleges, the state university was to provide scholarships for three years of study by poor but worthy students. To have had to pay for college and university scholarships of poor boys may seem like an undue financial burden for the people of Virginia, but Jefferson's academic standards for scholarships were very high. Also, there were only about twenty poor students from the primaries who could have scholarships in the colleges—Jefferson planned on having only one bright student from each of the twenty primaries selected for grammar school scholarships.

After a probationary period of two or three years in the college, many students would be failed and dropped. Those remaining would be able to continue for another six years and of these about twenty were expected to survive. Jefferson meant for the combined graduating group from all the colleges of Virginia to be about twenty. Half of these, about ten men, would be encouraged to go on to the University of William and Mary.

Jefferson did not consider cost when limiting matriculation at the University. His figures were based on available talent and nothing else. He was set against the then popular British belief that cost-free schooling always is pure charity. "It is a necessity for the Republican form of government," said Jefferson, "never is it philanthropy." When confronted with the question of whether it was right to take away the property of the more wealthy for the education of the children of others, Jefferson told the propertied men that free schooling was all to their advantage. The benefit to the rich man of free primaries would be "the peopling of his neighborhood with honest, useful, and enlightened citizens, understanding their own rights, and firm in their perpetuation." True, Jefferson went on to argue, only a few constituted "the natural aristocracy of talent and virtue." But many were able to profit from the primaries, and though

Jefferson wished to "cull the aristocracy of talent and virtue," he felt that the primaries were more important than the University. This must have been true, for he wrote Cabell:

> Were it necessary to give up either the Primaries or the University I would rather abandon the last, because it is safer to have a whole people respectably enlightened, than a few in a high state of science, and the many in ignorance. This last is the most dangerous state in which a nation can be. The nations and government of Europe are so many proofs of it (1:71).

A second reading of this passage reaffirms the opinion that Jefferson's endorsement of the primaries was borne up by his confidence in human nature. He truly felt that all men could become "honest, useful, and enlightened citizens, understanding their own rights, and firm in their perpetuation." And all this as a consequence of three years of primary instruction! Only well-endowed men could get so much from primary schools.

LATER FORCES THAT MADE FOR AN EXTENSION
OF EDUCATIONAL OPPORTUNITY:
THE DEMANDS OF ORGANIZED LABOR

Labor unions and other groups of industrial workers in the United States demanded public education for the children of urban workers by mid-nineteenth century. Farmers, where organized, were no less interested in education for their children, though they were less effective in making their votes count. One of the first demands of unions was for "equal, universal education." When the cities swelled with immigrants, only a "common school" could make them citizens recognizably American; those who knew no English had to become literate, or at least their children did, if the American economy was not to be held back. But the forces opposing the extension of free, public education were strong. In addition to the argument that it was wrong to take one man's money for the education of another man's children, the public schools were charged with being "Godless" because they were nonsectarian. Horace Mann (1796-1859), first state superintendent of schools in the United States, was unsparingly attacked by Protestant divines for being the proponent of a school that was without religion and therefore a threat to the morals of the young. Catholics joined in the criticism on the ground that no public school supported from the general revenue and controlled by a secular state could legally teach any sectarian religion. Without such sectarian religion, the Catholic criticism held, there could be no firm foundation for moral instruction, and children would be injured by the lack of ethical, as well as religious, instruction.

Horace Mann fought back, and the fight enlisted the strength of many as devout as the attackers. European observers could not but have been amazed for they had no similar struggle. Kings and elder statesmen had decided that a minimum of instruction was necessary for the health and strength of the state, and not until late in the nineteenth century was there militant European leadership that pressed for an extension of educational opportunity to the masses as having the right to send their children to free elementary and vocational schools.

In New England, where pressure for education had been evident from early Colonial days, there were the insistent speeches and publications of Horace Mann in Massachusetts and of Henry Barnard, also a state superintendent, in Connecticut. All along the eastern seaboard the argument for public education preoccupied press and forum. But the largest number of leaders in the "common school movement," as it was called, were from the West. In the backwoods country, on the prairie, and across the Rockies in California there were men who knew well the common people and their desires, their need for public schools. The western roster was long: John Sweet in California; Calvin Stowe, Samuel Galloway, and Samuel Lewis in Ohio; Caleb Mills in Indiana; Edwards in Illinois; Breckinridge in Kentucky; John D. Pierce and Issac Crary in Michican.

As the controversy moved to its climax in the Kalamazoo decision of 1874, no one could fail to see that at the very foundation of a system of public education was the legality of using tax monies for the support of the schools. There had been federal funds for public schools ever since 1785, when the land ordinance of that year provided that the sixteenth section of every township (nearly a square mile) should be reserved for sale or lease "for the maintenance of public schools within the said township." Two years later, this principle was restated in Article 3 of the Northwest Ordinance, which read: "Religion, morality, and knowledge, being necessary to good government and happiness of mankind, schools and the means of education shall forever be encouraged." But if the responsibility for, and control of, public education were to be lodged in the communities and capitals of each state, local and state taxes would have to support schools. When the right to levy and use these monies was assured—and it was before the end of the nineteenth century—there was no longer any doubt as to the pattern of organization of public education which is now to be found in the United States.

It only remained for the states to pass laws compelling school attendance in public or private schools, and after compulsory attendance laws were secured, to organize a professional cadre to organize and staff the state systems. In 1852, Massachusetts led the nation in passing a state-wide compulsory attendance law; by 1900 thirty-two states had followed suit, and by 1920 all states in the United States had compulsory attendance laws. Legislation forbidding child labor was a natural partner of compulsory attendance, but such is the greed of men that as late as 1920 the United States census reported a million children ten to fifteen years of age "gainfully employed."

For reasons that are not altogether clear, vocational training fared better in Europe during the nineteenth century than it did in the United States. Perhaps the reason for cooler American attitudes was the rejection of the notion of vocational training being education appropriate to youngsters of a lower socio-economic class. In a country, most of whose political leaders responded to the popular belief in equalitarianism, anything that smacked of social-class distinctions was put aside.

In 1880, however, manual training as a portion of general education got its foot in the door. It was then that Professor Calvin M. Woodward opened his manual training high school in St. Louis. It was a four-year school whose curriculum included the study of the use of tools and mechanical drawing, side-by-side with conventional courses in mathematics, science, literature, and language (24:72).

The modern concept of industrial arts education was heir to manual training, and the philosopher of education who best understood the unique opportunities presented by industrial arts education was John Dewey (1859-1952). Dewey's little book, *School and Society* (1900), pointed out that no one could be thought educated who did not understand that modern society would be molded by industrialization, technology, and capitalism. While Dewey did not go so far as to recommend that young people come to know more of economics, he did urge that all be given a chance to appreciate the transformation of society by industrialization.

Dewey's thought, like Woodward's, was not bent toward special vocational training. The only schools that were wholly given for the purpose of vocational training were "industrial schools for poor and delinquent children." Also, correctional institutions often had shops, but vocational instruction was auxiliary to the central purpose of reform. Not until the first quarter of the nineteenth century did the United States see even a glimmer of what vocational education might become. It was 1824 before the first technical institute was opened in Troy, New York ". . . to give instruction to the sons and daughters of farmers and mechanics in the application of experimental chemistry, philosophy and natural history to agriculture, domestic economy, and the arts of manufacture" (24:113-14). The Rensselaer School took on added distinction with the passing years, and is now one of the leading graduate schools of engineering science. The historical development of the Rensselaer Polytechnical Institute into a graduate school of engineering sciences is an excellent example of the evolution that has taken place in technology.

The mechanical arts institutes were followed by various schools of vocational training supported by manufacturers. Private proprietary schools mushroomed (24:115). But it took the need for skilled labor, made manifest by World War I, to win from Congress federal support of vocational education; the Smith-Hughes Act became law in February, 1917, inaugurating a succession of enactments that reimbursed states for the teaching of vocational agriculture, home economics, and industrial arts.

In Europe the course was differently run. In France and Prussia, the closing years of the eighteenth century saw the first stirrings of national government's interest in primary education. Napoleon appreciated the value of a national system of schools prepared to graduate loyal citizens, and his decrees of 1808 lodged education firmly in the hands of the central government—a model for all of Europe. But it was not till 1833 that France actually undertook the creation of public elementary schools. The Guizot Law of 1833 really accomplished little, and France had a national system of elementary education only after 1881.

In England, philanthropic individuals had agitated during the first quarter of the nineteenth century for charity toward the children of the very poor. These religious idealists acted through the British and Foreign School Society or the National Society for Promoting the Education of the Poor in the Principles of the Established Church. In 1833, the British government was moved to assist in the building of elementary schools, under pressure from these social reformers, whose power was at its height at this time. Twenty thousand pounds was voted for the erection of school-houses for the education of poor children. Not till the Elementary Education Act of 1870, however, was there anything approaching useful support for a national system of elementary education. Even then public enthusiasm was modest, though greater than that for the support of secondary schools, which made their debut with the Technical Instruction Act of 1889 and the Local Taxation Act of 1890. These acts made it possible for British districts to levy taxes for the support of secondary education, but the levies were anything but large.

On the Continent, the stages of growth through which public elementary and secondary education moved roughly paralleled those of England. Everywhere it became clear that there were to be these two distinct school systems, everywhere, that is, but in Great Britain. The English developed a unique method of furnishing separate schools for the upper and lower classes—a method that influenced both the United States and Canada. The British had public elementary and secondary schools by the First

91

World War, but side-by-side with them were private schools whose high tuition kept out the children of the lower classes, except for a handful brought in on scholarships. In the remainder of Europe no large-scale systems of private schools developed once the national governments took a genuine interest in education. Cynics have said that this was because the governments did not wish private schools that might teach students anything disloyal. Whether this was the controlling reason or not, private schools did not flourish on the Continent. Social classes were separated in schools, however, but it must not be thought that the upper classes planned the separation. They and the lower classes took it for granted, as class differences came to be taken for granted after the Middle Ages.

Lower-class children attended public elementary schools from four to six years. By 1914, it was not uncommon for many of these youngsters to continue their elementary education for a year or two longer in so-called "higher elementary schools" or "continued elementary education." In Germany, some graduated from the elementary schools to a "middle school," and then rejoined the other lower- or middle-class youngsters who had been enrolled in vocational schools after finishing elementary school. In all countries, vocational schools awaited the great majority of graduates from the elementary schools.

Children of upper middle- and upper-class families in Europe attended elementary schools that prepared them for the humanistic secondary schools preparatory for entrance to the universities. Even if these children enrolled in the same elementary schools as the lower-class children, they left their friends when it came time to enter a secondary school. Most lower-class youngsters went to vocational schools; only a few were bound for the universities.

One of the myths that Americans learn about European education is that only the children of the upper classes attend the universities. Once European nations adopted the principle of limiting attendance at the universities to those who passed the comprehensive examinations at the end of secondary school, it was inevitable that some upper-class children would fail of admission. The percentage of those who failed mounted with each decade because universities did not grow in size with the increase in population. This is not to deny that, speaking, relatively fewer of the lower-class than upper-class youth attempt to attend the preparatory secondary schools of the universities.

THE REFORM OF EDUCATION
IN THE RECENT PAST

England took the lead in the changes in European education that came after World War II. The British passed their Butler Act in 1944, an act whose provisions were all but revolutionary. The opening section of the Act contained a general statement of principle, calling for educational opportunity for all in terms of their abilities and interests. No longer was a bright and ambitious student to be kept from a college-preparatory education because he could not afford the tuition of a private grammar school. The Act called for the provision of public grammar schools for all who were academically qualified. Further, the Butler Act created *technical* secondary schools, as well as "modern schools" for all those whose examinations, taken toward the end of elementary school (the "eleven-plus" examinations), were not passed with high enough grades to merit admission to a grammar or technical school.

While no European country has been able to win "parity of esteem" for all schooling, academic, humanistic, and vocational, it will not be long before Europe has moved away from separate schools for the upper and lower classes. In 1950, Sweden broke the tradition of separate schools, and today all children in that Scandinavian democracy attend the same school for the first nine years of their formal education. In advanced secondary schools, some move into vocational programs and others go on to technical and professional training. But till the age of sixteen, all have been together.

BIBLIOGRAPHY

1. ARROWOOD, CHARLES F., ed., *Thomas Jefferson and Education in the Republic.* New York: McGraw-Hill Book Company, Inc., 1930.
2. BARKER, ERNEST, GEORGE CLARK, and P. VAUCHER, *The European Inheritance,* Vol. II. Oxford: The Clarendon Press, 1954.
3. BENNETT, CHARLES A., *History of Manual and Industrial Education up to 1870.* Peoria, Ill.: The Manual Arts Press, 1926.
4. ———, *History of Manual and Industrial Education, 1870-1914.* Peoria, Ill.: The Manual Arts Press, 1937.
5. BUTTS, R. FREEMAN, *A Cultural History of Western Education.* New York: McGraw-Hill Book Company, Inc., 1955.
6. ——— and LAWRENCE A. CREMIN, *A History of Education in American Culture.* New York: Holt, Rinehart & Winston, Inc., 1953.
7. CHANNING, EVA, trs., Pestalozzi's *Leonard and Gertrude.* Boston: Ginn & Company, 1885.
8. CLOUGH, SHEPARD B. and CHARLES W. COLE, *Economic History of Europe.* Boston: D. C. Heath & Company, 1952.
9. COOKE, EBENEZER, ed., LUCY E. HOLLAND, and FRANCIS C. TURNER, trs., *How Gertrude Teaches Her Children,* by J. H. Pestalozzi. Syracuse, N. Y.: C. W. Bardeen, 1898.
10. CREMIN, LAWRENCE A., ed., *The Republic and the School: Horace Mann on the Education of Free Men.* New York: Columbia University Press, 1957.
11. CUBBERLY, ELLWOOD P., *Public Education in the United States.* Boston: Houghton Mifflin Company, 1934.
12. DRAKE, WILLIAM E., *The American School in Transition.* Englewood Cliffs, N. J.: Prentice-Hall, Inc., 1955.

13. EBY, FREDERICK, *The Development of Modern Education*. Englewood Cliffs, N. J.: Prentice-Hall, Inc., 1952.

14. FONTAINERIE, F. DE LA, *French Liberalism and Education in the Eighteenth Century*. New York: McGraw-Hill Book Company, Inc., 1932.

15. FOXLEY, BARBARA, trs., *Émile*, by Jean Jacques Rousseau. New York: E. P. Dutton & Co., Inc., 1933.

16. FRANKLIN, BENJAMIN, *Proposals for the Education of the Youth in Pennsylvania, 1749*. Ann Arbor: The William L. Clements Library, 1927.

17. GREEN, J. A., *Pestalozzi's Educational Writings*. New York: David McKay Co., Inc., 1912.

18. KANDEL, I. L., *Comparative Education*. Boston: Houghton Mifflin Company, 1933.

19. ———, *The New Era in Education*. Boston: Houghton Mifflin Company, 1955.

20. KIRKLAND, EDWARD C., *A History of American Economic Life*. New York: Appleton-Century-Crofts, Inc., 1951.

21. MEYER, ADOLPHE E., *An Educational History of the American People*. New York: McGraw-Hill Book Company, Inc., 1957.

22. PARSONS, TALCOTT, trs., *The Protestant Ethic and the Spirit of Capitalism*, by Max Weber. London: George Allen & Unwin, Ltd., 1930.

23. PRESNELL, L. S., ed., *Studies in the Industrial Revolution*. London: The Athlone Press, 1960.

24. ROBERTS, ROY W., *Vocational and Practical Arts Education*. New York: Harper & Row, Publishers, 1957.

25. SPENCER, HERBERT, *Education*. New York: Appleton-Century-Crofts, Inc., 1881.

26. TAWNEY, RICHARD H., *Equality*. London: George Allen & Unwin, 1931.

27. ———, *Religion and the Rise of Capitalism*. New York: Harcourt, Brace & World, Inc., 1926.

28. TREVELYAN, G. M., *Illustrated English Social History*, Vol. II. London: Longmans, Green, & Company, Ltd., 1950.

29. WOODY, THOMAS, ed., *Educational Views of Benjamin Franklin*. New York: McGraw-Hill Book Company, Inc., 1931.

Today, in the United States, professional students of education tend increasingly to work as scientists; in the future, this trend surely will not be reversed. The prosperity now enjoyed by the scientific study of education has been earned; what it promises for the future is promised with confidence, although as a branch of science it is among the newest. Before the 1880's there was little that could have been described as scientific about the treatment of questions of educational administration, instruction, or the process of learning. In the years since, however, there has appeared a flood of research. Some of this research has been experimental, aimed at determining the results of new techniques of teaching, and so forth. More of it has taken the form of "status studies" —inquiries into the relations of variables, such as age, to ability to learn. These relational studies not only have been typical of status studies in general, they have proved that advances in measurement and statistics have been essential to the development of a scientific study of education.

95

THE SCIENTIFIC STUDY OF EDUCATION

8

Determining the relations of variables was made possible in the late nineteenth century by Karl Pearson's mathematical construct, the "product moment correlation coefficient," used by another Englishman, Galton, to elaborate on the concept of correlation between forces, factors, or anything measurable.

That so many useful scientific studies was made must be credited first to improvements in the techniques of observation, measurement, and statistical analysis, made between 1890 and 1910. The rapidly maturing science of psychology, teamed with the improved techniques of inquiry, hastened the development of a scientific study of education.

This development began in Germany early in the nineteenth century with the career of Johann Friedrich Herbart (18:Chap. 18). Herbart (1776-1841) was both a philosopher and psychologist, though his psychology would hardly be classed as such today. It was speculative psychology, an effort to develop a comprehensive, consistent, and coherent explanation of such things as the human mind and will. Herbart had no evidence for his speculation; it was conjecture, as all preceding philosophic thought on these subjects had been. But educators in Europe and the United States honored Herbart as the leading scientific thinker of the century on education.

Toward the end of Herbart's life, however, a boy was born in Germany who was radically to reconstruct psychology, substituting laboratory experiments for speculation. Wilhelm Max Wundt (1832-1926) inaugurated the scientific study of sensation and perception. His American students included G. Stanley Hall (1846-1924), originator of child study and the psychological study of adolescence and senility, James McKeen Cattell (1860-1944), father of the American "measurement movement" in education, and Charles Judd (1873-1946), a third pundit in the new scientific study of education.

There were other influences of the first magnitude playing on the new science. In England, Sir Francis Galton (1822-1911), innovator in the new science of eugenics, turned the mathematics of Karl Pearson to use in devising quantitative units of measurement of deviation in differences between and within groups. It had been the research of Charles Darwin, a cousin, that had drawn Galton's attention to the importance of deviations or variations, both between individuals and within groups. Galton's interest was not only in variations or differences that aided or hindered survival, but in precise measures of those deviations. His publications featured curves to express the manner in which individuals were distributed when surveyed in terms of their height, weight, or any other trait.

The research of Pearson and Galton became known in the United States through the teaching and publications of James McKeen Cattell, who studied with Wundt in Leipzig and with Galton in London. After his return to the United States, Cattell was installed as a professor of psychology at Columbia University, where he had as his most famous student Edward Lee Thorndike (1874-1949), who became the most potent American force in both general and educational psychology.

In France, Alfred Binet (1857-1911) lent his name to the best-remembered early scientific research on education. For ten years he and his collaborator, Simon, studied to create an instrument to measure intelligence. The results, published in 1905 and revised twice before Binet died, were the first versions of the intelligence tests that became a household word a generation later. Most Americans were unfamiliar with the Simon-Binet test till 1916, however, when Lewis Terman published the Stanford Revision of the Simon-Binet test.

These pioneers in the sciences that first nourished the scientific study of education operated in laboratories, with reasonable precise measures and statistics. One who did not was a physician in Italy, Dr. Maria Montessori (1870-1952), the first woman to graduate as a physician from the University of Rome. She enters into the history of education as a pioneer in applying to the teaching of the young implications of studies in physical anthropology and studies on the mentally and socially retarded. Her publications and teachings led to conclusions on how the three R's might be taught to very young children. The interest of Americans in Montessori between 1911 and 1915 was so great as to amount almost to a cult.

Montessori thought of herself as a scientist, but the history of education has numbered neither her nor the imaginative Swiss educator, Adolphe Ferrière, among scientists. The reason for this simply has been the decision that the scientific study of education shall include only experimental research of status studies, using modern theory and techniques both of measurement and statistical design and analysis.

JOHANN FRIEDRICH HERBART

For those whose careers are devoted to promoting student learning, the scientific study of education can be most useful when productive of insights into the more effective means of motivating learning, prompting understanding as well as creative thinking, and improving the chances for remembering what is learned in a fashion that renders knowledge useful. Among those who dominate the studies in this general area of human learning, there has been a conflict between those who emphasize the teachings of the associationists (Herbart, Thorndike, and Thorndike's successors) and those who favor functionalist theories whose champion was John Dewey and many others who stressed the power of purpose and (unlike Dewey) emotions, values, and attitudes. Today, the two camps have moved to close ranks; it would be difficult to point to a pure functionalist or a pure associationist. For many years, however, this reconciliation seemed remote.

The associationists held sway for quite a time. Theirs was a common-sense position. To conceive of memories in terms of Bain's "beaten tracks" in the brain was but a step from the connections between ideas as described by John Locke in the seventeenth century. But it was an obvious manner of conception, for after all, men tended to follow beaten tracks in the world. It was easy and natural to conceive of the brain as furnished with its own byways for handling the traffic of ideas. New ideas were thought to carve out new paths; old and oft-repeated ideas were imagined to whiz along deeply grooved paths. It was a simple, mechanistic view.

When Herbart came on the scene, many philosophers were willing to accept John Locke's thesis that impressions received by the mind were associated with one another because of such mechanical factors as their being similar. Ideas were said to be born of these impressions in association. The idea of red, for example, was imagined to grow from many impressions of redness. The implications of this for educators, of course, was that an idea, to be firmly fixed in the mind, must be presented many times. It was as though Quintilian's stress on the primacy of memory among the faculties was being given scientific sanction. Herbart took seriously the problems of teaching, even though he was the leading academic philosopher of his country. He laid out precise instructions for teachers as to how to build a student's store of knowledge. The "Herbartian steps" became the precepts of teacher training for several generations (19).

The theory upon which the steps rested was itself based on the conception of the mind as an "apperceptive mass," new ideas sticking with old ones which were related to them. Herbart believed that impressions and ideas actually had an interest in and an attraction for similar ideas and impressions. A student was held to be interested in concepts related to those already mastered. The careful teacher saw to it that this interest was exploited. Leaving nothing to chance, Herbart outlined the five steps that comprised teaching: preparation, presentation, association, generalization, and application.

In preparation, the teacher tried to see to it that memories, or anything that could be connected with the topic about to be studied, were recalled to the consciousness of the students. Step two, presentation, consisted in making certain that the students understood the new materials. Here Herbart followed the suggestion of Pestalozzi and Comenius. Teachers were urged to find concrete illustrations of any abstract ideas to be learned. In the third step of method, that of association, the assimilation of the new ideas into the apperceptive mass took place. It was shown how the new and the old ideas could be compared—how they were alike and how they differed. When the new ideas had been made clear to the students, they saw that many ideas could be related to it and that generalization must be possible. In the last step, application, the ideas learned were to help students interpret new experiences.

Stripped of the underlying theory, Herbart's suggestions on method were a vast improvement on anything available to teachers in the nineteenth century. As a consequence, Herbart enjoyed the greatest repute abroad, and in the United States it did not take long for the practicality of what Herbart taught to catch on. So many educators were attracted that in 1895 a National Herbart Society was established in the United States; anyone who was anybody in education belonged. There were college presidents, including Nicholas Murray Butler of Columbia University, and there was John Dewey, who was beginning to make his presence felt as a leader in educational thought. Everyone rallied around the Society, which promised to be the center of research addressed to the improvement of education.

Within a very few years, the National Herbart Society was defunct. Those of its members who remained devoted to research aimed at the improvement of instruction formed a new body, the National Society for the Scientific Study of Education. Today, the same organization flourishes as the National Society for the Study of Education. The term *scientific* has been dropped from its masthead, perhaps because the study of education has become so clearly the province of scientists that their monopoly is taken for granted, at least by themselves.

JOHN DEWEY (1859-1952)

The passing of the National Herbart Society was not attributable solely to the ascendency of experimental science over philosophy. At the time of the breakup of the National Herbart Society, the rejection of Herbart's theory was on the grounds of its rather mechanical associationism and the devastating effects of a blind devotion to his five steps in teaching (11).

John Dewey's slashing attacks on Herbart gave American Herbartianism its *coup de grâce*. Dewey effectively disputed both Herbart's description of the human mind (and human learning) and what was implied by his five formal steps of teaching.

"Herbartianism seems to me essentially a schoolmaster's psychology, not the psychology of a child," said Dewey of Herbart's outlook (13). It was meant to be a harsh judgment, for Dewey had come to the conclusion, after discussion with such trained observers of teaching as his friend Colonel Francis W. Parker, that in a class taught by Herbartian technique all the work was being done by the teacher. He controlled everything. *He* did the clarifying entailed in the first two steps of preparation. It was a teacher-centered classroom. More accurately, it was teacher-and-subject-centered. The student really had to do nothing but learn!

Herbart would not have agreed with Bain; he held mind to be distinct from the rest of the organism. In the classic philosophical tradition, Herbart's view became classed as the "mind-body dualism." For the better part of sixty years, Dewey wrote and lectured against this dualism. His view has been known as the "naturalistic" and "monistic" interpretation of mind and learning. Monism has led to the wedding of mind and body. Naturalism really signaled the same thing.

The naturalism of Dewey was biological (2), but it is not simply that; it was also *Darwinian*. This meant that Dewey riveted his attention on the means that men had available for survival, as seen in their solving of the problems posed them. The essential fact of Dewey's belief was that man can *progress* if he uses his natural intelligence and his experience with the past in solving problems. In Dewey's functionalist version of the mind, the mind was triggered by the organism's interest in its own purposes, its problems. The implication of this for teachers was that they should give students practice in solving problems rather than simply in remembering and reciting.

Functionalism. The essential difference between Herbart's associationist (or any later version) and Dewey's functionalist blueprint of mind and intelligence lies in Herbart's acceptance of a dualism of body and mind. Also, Dewey rejected the view that made mind a product of the interaction of sensations and ideas that come to it from the environment (or teacher), no role being played by the purposes or lively interests of the human being.

Dewey describes men essentially as organisms of infinite complexity, organisms which had evolved perhaps as Darwin had pictured. Certainly, he thought, they owed their success and progress to intelligence. To Dewey, intelligence meant the ability to use experience. When he became specific and described what he would consider an intelligent approach to solving a problem, his description sounded very much like a scientific approach to a problem.

This equating of intelligence with scientific method was not enough to tie Dewey into the science of education movement. This was accomplished by his work on psychology which was published in 1887. In his *Psychology*, Dewey revealed that he had become associated with a new, American school of psychology, *functionalism*. William James, the philosopher-physician-psychologist, was functionalism's most reputed proponent and the chief stimulus for Dewey's thinking. From this time forward, Dewey was to stand fast on the doctrine that mind is an organic function that man employs to reduce his drives, satisfy his needs, solve his problems, reach his goals, or be intelligent—all of these meant pretty much the same thing to Dewey. Life, as Dewey saw it, was *interaction* within an environment. The environment supplied men with cues and problems, and the human nervous system functioned to interpret the cues effectively enough for the problems to be valued and satisfactory solutions attained. He also had something quite important to say about the nature of the interaction; the experiences men undergo within their environment become the materials out of which they make meanings, the materials upon which they base their actions and plans. Clearly, the man Dewey envisioned was active and pursued his life interests. He was no creature of habit only, but spurred by his purposes into a dynamic interaction with an environment that changed enough to present him always with alternatives to challenge his intelligence.

How We Think. In 1910, Dewey published a little book titled *How We Think* (11), listing five steps in thinking which Dewey offered to teachers as substitutes for the five steps of teaching described by Herbart. Dewey asked teachers to replace teaching students ideas and acts with encouraging them to think or solve problems.

Dewey's first step concerned the realization on the *part of the student* that there was a problem, that he faced a problematic situation. When things became obscure, Dewey felt, the pupil sensed a need for clarification which became his interest and, for Dewey, the tense innerspring of driving motivation. The student now had a purpose. In the second step, the problem was tackled, inspected thoroughly on all sides, and hopefully understood. In step three, ways were suggested by which the problem might be solved; *hypotheses were to be drawn and tested experimentally.* The fourth step only extended the hypothesizing. Dewey did not expect the student to jump directly from the first guess to its trial. Only the more likely hypotheses were to be tested. In step four, the guesses or hypotheses were to be culled. In the fifth step, the most likely hypotheses were to be put to the test. Failure would presumably lead to a repetition of the last four steps. Success or failure would provide experience on which to base later thought.

EDWARD LEE THORNDIKE

Dewey, in essence, was asking teachers to permit their students to follow naturally the habitual use of scientific method in problem-solving. But Dewey was not looked upon as a scientist himself, but rather as a philosopher. Herbart may have been driven from the field, but a new group of associationists, the Thorndikians, arose and their patron, Edward Lee Thorndike, enjoyed the most impeccable reputation as a scientist.

While his theories on how associative bonds are built and how the mind is formed were noteworthy elements in Thorndike's general psychology, educators were as much impressed with his experimental studies on mental discipline. Though we will say no more on the subject, it is easy to imagine the force carried by Thorndike's conclusion that neither Latin nor mathematics was superior for disciplining the mind in general (42). He concluded, rather, that educational objectives should be stated in terms of specific skills, insights, or attitudes considered desirable for students to master, and then that highly specific drill and subject matter should be devised to promote the learning desired. There was no evidence, Thorndike thought, for any such power as a disciplined mind in general. People could learn to do a great many specific things, and they required the *appropriate* specific subject matter and academic exercises—including practice, memorization, or drill.

S-R bond psychology and behaviorism. Among the assumptions of Thorndike's "connectionism," as it was called, was that all learning is a matter of connections between responses and their stimuli. The imaginative study of conditioning forwarded by the Russian physiologist-psychologist, Pavlov, gave rise to the popularly known form of the equation Learning-Stimulus-Response, i.e., if stimulus A is found to be associated with Response Q, repeat A until Q appears without hesitation whenever A is present.

Teachers were soon made aware of Thorndike's equation. To many, it meant that drill and repetition were not only useful, but the most useful devices for instructing. Little place was left for the purposes of students. The understanding, the interest, the relevance of materials—all now played a secondary role.

In the early 1920's, behaviorism was born of connectionism. It was the logical extreme of associationist thinking. The name that was linked with behaviorism was that of John B. Watson (1878-1958), who published *Behavior* in 1914 (44). Watson was an heir to associationism, coming into its tradition as a consequence of adopting the conditioning theory of Pavlov and the connectionism of Thorndike. Watson claimed that environment (stimuli or conditioning) makes the man. Any baby could be raised to be a thief or a professional man. This was possible because heredity was far less important than environment. Setting aside the question of striking a balance between environment and heredity, the behavioristic theory of learning showed a strikingly associationist character in the assumption that learning is simply a matter of what *happens to the learner.*

THE OBJECTIONS OF THE FUNCTIONALISTS

Dewey and those who shared his beliefs thought as little of behaviorism as they did of connectionism, Herbartianism, and other refinements of associationism (28). To them, behaviorism and connectionism were but two more dualistic theories. The learner was held apart from the environment, yet he was seen as the passive recipient of lessons, of stimuli, of prodding from the teacher, from the environment. Functionalism rejected the notion that man as learner was passive, soaking up influences from the environment or the cultural heritage. The functionalist would not accept the idea of man being creative in everything *but in learning.* Why, they seemed to ask, should the teacher be thought of as active and the student, because a learner, passive?

There was no issue over the fact of the teacher, the adult, knowing more than the student, nor was there an issue over the value of the cultural heritage. The sole point of difference from the associationist tradition, ancient and modern, was over the role of the living purposes of the student, which the functionalists saw to be the true motives for learning. They looked for these purposes in the life a student lived, which meant that they had to inquire into the *needs* felt by the learner as a seven year old child living in such and such a place, for instance. They looked to the individual for a clue as to what motives he might have that could be tapped, and they asked that teachers do the same for each individual student. They did not wish the teacher to *ask* the student what he was interested in; they asked the teacher to learn about the individual, to gauge what he might become interested in doing.

THE SCIENTIFIC STUDY OF THE CHILD

Although some observations on the nature of childhood and adolescence are very old, the scientific study of child development grew out of the early 1920's. The art of instruction has only begun to profit from application without a clear recognition of individual differences in capacity and development. The wealth of harvest to come was forecast by John Anderson, looking back to the middle of the nineteenth century when all that was known of children and youth was the fruit of common sense and keen observation (3:182). In retrospect, Anderson saw his predecessors in education without a clear recognition of individual differences in capacity and growth, without an understanding of how human beings learn to adjust.

Late in the nineteenth century, it was possible to see such men as Bryan and Harter (3:182) preparing the way for experimental studies of methods for improving instruction and learning. Both were interested in upgrading the performance of telegraphists, and carefully plotted the curve of improvement with practice. They did not propose experiments with alternative methods of facilitating progress, but their studies were an invitation to just such experimentation. William James performed the pioneer experiment on what is for educators the all-important subject of transfer of training. Did learning in any subject, logic for example, help one to be generally logical in life? Did learning to be accurate in the woodworking shop transfer to increase the accuracy with which one performed in other connections?

A great deal of experimentation was inspired by the functionalist-associationist controversy, and one of the indirect benefits of the controversy was the strengthening of the case for settling questions in education by experimentation, *where experimental study was relevant*. There would always be differences of opinion on such matters as that of merit of introducing the teaching of religion in public schools, or of the purposes of education in general—issues to which experimental study could not provide clues to possible answers. But for matters open to experimental study, a new tool of great power was being forged.

A most important event occurred in the first decade of this century

103

(3:182-183). In 1907, Alfred Binet undertook to rescue children who had been institutionalized as feeble-minded without the benefit of objective indices of handicap. His research reached fruition in the publication of scales, relating certain levels of performance with age. Binet's studies offered compelling evidence that children's performance increases rapidly with age, and more important, that measurable differences in mental level affected a child's achievement in school. Moreover, Binet's measures were quantitative; children were not judged intuitively.

The excitement that Binet's studies generated was kept alive by Thorndike's massive schedule of research on a host of topics of the highest importance to teachers. Transfer of training was but one area of Thorndike's inquiry. His more basic contribution was in improving statistical and measurement techniques, without which experimental research could not be designed, nor the results of research interpreted and generalized. Applying these tools, Thorndike and his associates and pupils found out the content of children's vocabularies at all ages. Very little that could be measured, was left unmeasured, and perhaps some things were measured that were incapable of being stated in terms of quantitative units.

Between 1900 and 1915, the scientific study of education in the United States matured. More than any other single factor contributing to this growing up was the improvement in techniques of measurement and experimentation.

> In this period were developed various statistical formulas, achievement tests, intelligence tests, and techniques of experimental control. . . . In addition, these instruments, techniques, and procedures were employed in valuating the effectiveness of educational programs of organized research. . . . (38:1147)

Between 1915 and 1935, testing and measuring in education were tremendously productive and useful. Then, in 1935 and for the next few years (38:1147), B. O. Smith and others raised fundamental questions about the presuppositions that might be attributed to those who were associated with the test—measurement movement, but there was little fruitful discussion, for too few were equipped to meet Smith in the field of the logical foundations of measurement. Those who tested and measured had no time for the inspection of the logical ground on which they stood.

The new measurement techniques were tried out on adults, the American volunteers and draftees of World War I. Hundreds of psychologists were trained in the techniques, and after the war were scattered throughout the United States, carrying far and wide the new scientific study of measurable differences between human beings. Not all that the psychologists found in surveying the young Americans entering their nation's service was encouraging. Many were illiterate, had correctable physical defects, or were maladjusted. All too many had intellectual capacities the schools had not challenged.

In order to find remedies for these situations, it was necessary to have both reliable knowledge of how children grow and develop and knowledge of how this development might be aided (3:184). The first organized research institute to make studies of child growth and development opened in 1917 as Iowa's Child Welfare Research Station. Then, in the early twenties, the world had one of its first glimpses at what a great foundation could do to advance scholarship. The Laura Spelman Rockefeller Memorial, guided by Beardsley Ruml and Lawrence K. Frank, made large sums of money available for encouraging research in child development and parent education. These monies made possible the opening of the Child Welfare Institute at Teachers College, Columbia University, in 1924, and openings of similar institutes at the University of California in 1927. The scientific study of all phases of child growth and development was assured. From the steadily enlarging pool of research, elementary schooling was to become more effective because instructional methods and materials could be systematically and carefully improved.

THE SCIENTIFIC STUDY OF ADOLESCENCE: "EMOTIONS AND THE EDUCATIVE PROCESS"

In order that the high school be similarly strengthened, it was mandatory that a similar venture be launched into the period of adolescent growth and development. Although the two volumes of G. Stanley Hall's *Adolescence* appeared in 1904, the scientific study of adolescence remained dormant until the 1930's, when the needs of youth became a most lively topic of research and discussion. Perhaps the dilemma of young people without prospect of employment during the 1930's touched off the studies. The anxieties of so many of these adolescents commanded attention, and a commission of the Progressive Education Association engaged a trio of psychologists to make recommendations for the reorganization of secondary education, so that it could more adequately care for the needs of youth. One of the three, Caroline Zachry, was a leader in the field of mental hygiene; the scientific study of emotional development through adolescence, then, together with educational implications of that period, was put before the professional public.

Reorganizing Secondary Education (39) appeared in 1939. The year before, Prescott had published *Emotion and the Educative Process* (34), which had been commissioned by the American Council on Education; this book indicated a new awareness on the past of educators that adolescence had to be studied for the guidance of secondary education. The scientific study of childhood, which already was far advanced, had shown its value for the improvement of elementary schooling. Had not World War II intervened to disrupt all scientific study of adolescence and its application to teaching, research data might well have been spectacular during the 1950's. It was not, however, and the Forty-third Yearbook of the National Society for the Study of Education (1944) could report few fundamenal studies other than the initial moves made in the late 1930's.

Measuring academic achievement. Possibilities for progress in the scientific study of education, childhood, or adolescence depended upon valid and reliable instruments of measuring. These, in turn, required refinements in theories of measurement and statistics. These refinements came quickly. In 1890, James McKeen Cattell, first assistant to Wundt in Leipzig, published his *Mental Tests and Measurements.* One of Cattell's students, Thorndike, in less than a generation made the most significant contributions to the all-important field of scaling. Thorndike invented a "scale unit," to be used in measuring academic achievement. Using Thorndike's scale, a pupil said to be at the 80th percentile could be compared, in whatever was being measured, with any other student tested in the same area—arithmetic computation, for example. True, the effects on performance of such factors as the social class of the parents, the attitudes of the pupil, and other forces were not taken into account, but the foundations of a quantitative approach to education, an alternative to guessing and opinion, had been firmly nailed down (3:295). Cliff Stone, a student of Thorndike, produced the first objective test of achievement in arithmetic reasoning in 1908. Thorndike's own famous first scale to measure handwriting was read in 1909 and published the following year. "Its publication," wrote Meyer, "had generally been regarded as the real beginning of the movement to measure the products of education statistically" (31:295).

The measurement of academic achievement had come a long way since its initial appearance in the United States toward the end of the nineteenth century, when Dr. Joseph Rice, editor of the *Forum,* studied the achievement of pupils being drilled in spelling, and making the obvious types of comparison, reviewed the spelling of some 30,000 pupils taught in alternate ways in different parts of the country.

Scientific recognition of the group. In recent years, educators have become interested in research on the dynamics of instructional groups (25). These are the interactions that take place among students and between students and teacher in any classroom in any school. Sociologists interested in bureaucracies and large-scale organizations carried the analysis of groups to interrelationships within entire school systems. This recognition of the group was to education, hardly visible in the United States before World War II. Although European sociologists like Durkheim, Tönnies, and Weber by World War I had become fully aware of the field comprising the study of groups, psychology was not prepared to join with sociology in an inquiry into the psychodynamics of interaction within small and large groups. When cooperative research on the part of these two basic sciences of human behavior was attained, an enormous literature was created in Europe and the United States. By 1960, educators everywhere, including the Soviet Union, where the life of the group has been taken most seriously, were in a position to be the sophisticated partners of scientists of behavior in studying the effects of roles that might be played by teachers and students.

The research of Flanders (20), suggested in Part II of the Fifty-ninth Yearbook of the National Society for the Study of Education, has illustrated the utility to the teacher of becoming aware of effects of his behavior on student learning. Some teachers tend to dominate the classroom and talk far more than the students, some of whom vary their roles in terms of what is sensed to be appropriate. In terms of facilitating learning by students, study in group dynamics has commanded genuine scientific interest as one of the most promising of the new tools for the scientific study of education.

BIBLIOGRAPHY

1. AIKIN, WILFORD M., *The Story of the Eight-year Study*. New York: Harper & Row, Publishers, 1942.

2. ALEXANDER, THOMAS and BERYL PARKER, *The New Education in the German Republic*. New York: The John Day Company, Inc., 1929.

3. ANDERSON, JOHN E., "Child Development: An Historical Perspective," *Child Development*, XXVII, No. 2 (1956), 181-196.

4. BAIN, ALEXANDER, *Education as a Science*. New York: Appleton-Century-Croft, Inc., 1881.

5. ———, *Mind and Body*. New York: Appleton-Century-Croft, Inc., 1897.

6. ———, *The Senses and the Intellect*. London: J. W. Parker and Sons, 1894.

7. BECK, ROBERT H., "Kilpatrick's Critique of Montessori's Method and Theory," *Studies in Philosophy and Education*, I, Nos. 4 and 5 (1961), 153-162.

8. COOK, WALTER W. and THEODORE CLYMER, "Acceleration and Retardation," in *Individualizing Instruction*, LXI, I (1962). Yearbook of the National Society for the Study of Education, ed. by Nelson B. Henry. Chicago: University of Chicago Press, 1962.

9. COOPER, FREDERICK T., trs., *Pedagogical Anthropology*, by Maria Montessori. New York: Frederick A. Stokes Company, 1913.

10. DAVIDSON, PERCY E., *The Recapitulation Theory and Human Infancy*. New York: Bureau of Publications, Teachers College, Columbia University, 1914.

11. DEWEY, JOHN, *How We Think*. Boston: D. C. Heath & Company, 1910.

12. ———, *The Influence of Darwin on Philosophy*. New York: Holt, Rinehart & Winston, Inc., 1910.

13. ———, "Interest as Related to Will," *Second Supplement to the Herbart Yearbook for 1895*. Chicago: University of Chicago Press, 1899.

14. DEWEY, JOHN, *Psychology*. New York: Harper & Row, Publishers, 1887.

15. ———, "The Reflex Arc Concept in Psychology," *Psychological Review*, III, No. 4 (1896), 357-370.

16. ———, *The Sources of a Science of Education*. New York: Horace Liveright, 1929.

17. DEWEY, JOHN and JAMES A. MC LELLAN, *The Psychology of Number and Its Application to Methods of Teaching Arithmetic*. New York: Appleton-Century-Crofts, Inc., 1895.

18. EBY, FREDERICK, *The Development of Modern Education*. Englewood Cliffs, N. J.: Prentice-Hall, Inc., 1952.

19. FELKIN, HENRY M. and EMMIE FELKIN, trs., *The Science of Education*, by Johann Friedrich Herbart. Boston: D. C. Heath & Company, 1902.

20. FLANDERS, NED A., "Diagnosing and Utilizing Social Structures in Classroom Learning," in *The Dynamics of Instructional Groups*, LIX, II (1960). National Society for the Study of Education, ed. by Nelson B. Henry. Chicago: University of Chicago Press, 1960.

21. GEORGE, ANNE E., trs., *The Montessori Method*, by Maria Montessori. New York: Frederick A. Stokes Company, 1912.

22. HAILMAN, W. N., trs., *The Education of Man*, by Friedrich Froebel. New York: Appleton-Century-Crofts, Inc., 1903.

23. HALL, GRANVILLE S., *Adolescence*. New York: Appleton-Century-Crofts, Inc., 1904.

24. HENRY, NELSON B., ed., *Adolescence*. XLIII, I (1944). National Society for the Study of Education. Chicago: University of Chicago Press, 1944.

25. ———, *The Dynamics of Instructional Groups*, LIX, II (1960). National Society for the Study of Education. Chicago: University of Chicago Press, 1960.

26. ———, *Individualizing Instruction*, LXI, X (1962). National Society for the Study of Education. Chicago: University of Chicago Press, 1962.

27. HILGARD, ERNEST R., *Theories of Learning*. New York: Appleton-Century-Crofts, Inc., 1956.

28. HULLFISH, H. GORDON, *Aspects of Thorndike's Psychology in Their Relation to Educational Theory and Practice*. Columbus: Ohio State University Press, n.d.

29. KILPATRICK, WILLIAM H., *The Montessori System Examined*. Boston: Houghton Mifflin Company, 1914.

30. MC CABE, JOSEPH, trs., *The Evolution of Man*, by Ernst H. P. A. Haeckel. New York: G. P. Putnam's Sons, 1910.

31. ———, *An Educational History of the American People*. New York: McGraw-Hill Book Co., Inc., 1957.

32. MEYER, ADOLPHE E., *Modern European Educators*. Englewood Cliffs, N. J.: Prentice-Hall, Inc., 1934.

33. MOORE, F. DEAN, trs., *The Activity School*, by Adolph Ferrière. New York: The John Day Company, Inc., 1928.

34. PRESCOTT, DANIEL A., *Emotion and the Educative Process*. Washington, D.C.: American Council on Education, 1938.

35. RICE, J. M., "The Futility of the Spelling Grind," *Forum*, XXIII. April (1897)

36. ROMAN, FREDERICK W., *The New Education in Europe*. New York: E. P. Dutton & Co., Inc., 1930.

37. SMITH, BUNNIE O., *Logical Aspects of Educational Measurement*. New York: The Macmillan Company, 1912.

38. ————, "Science of Education," *Encyclopedia of Educational Research*, Walter S. Monroe, ed. New York: The Macmillan Company, 1950.

39. THAYER, V. T., CAROLINE B. ZACHRY, and RUTH KOTINSKY, *Reorganizing Secondary Education*. New York: Appleton-Century-Crofts, Inc., 1939.

40. ————, *Education*. New York: The Macmillan Company, 1912.

41. THORNDIKE, EDWARD LEE, *Educational Psychology*. New York: Lemcke and Buechner, 1903.

42. ————, "Mental Discipline in High School Studies," *Journal of Educational Psychology*, XV, No. 1 (1924), 1-24; XV, No. 2 (1924), 83-98.

43. WASHBURNE, CARLETON and MYRON M. STEARNS, *New Schools in the Old World*. New York: The John Day Company, Inc., 1926.

44. WATSON, JOHN B., *Behavior*. New York: Holt, Rinehart & Winston, Inc., 1914

45. WHIPPLE, GUY M., ed., *The Scientific Movement in Education*, XXXVII, II (1938), The National Society for the Study of Education. Bloomington, Ill.: Public School Publishing Company, 1938.

46. ZACHRY, CAROLINE B. and MARGARET LIGHTY, *Emotion and Conduct in Adolescence*. New York: Appleton-Century-Crofts, Inc., 1940.

Between 1850 and 1950, education was modernized in western Europe and transformed in the United States, the United States following the European pattern in graduate and professional education. In 1857, when the National Teachers Association was organized, the nation was moving from a mercantile-agricultural economy to one primarily urban and industrial. Whereas in 1820 one-twentieth of the population of the United States was urban, one-sixth had become so by 1860, and one-third by 1900. The population grew prodigiously, trebling between 1820 and 1860. In that same period, coal production was multiplied 4,000 times, and pig iron production forty times. A great steel industry was about to be born. Cities grew from the influx of immigrants from Europe. In one ten-year period, 1845-1855, three million immigrants came to the United States. Nor did the rate of immigration decline appreciably before the first World War; between 1905 and 1910, a million immigrants a year asked for admission. The demands on the schools for programs of Americanization were obviously great.

THE
PROFESSIONALIZATION
OF TEACHING

9

The problems of the schools can be imagined not only in considering the scattering of families throughout the vast rural reaches of the country, but also in looking at the city slums, which grew as quickly as factories, and into which immigrant families were herded and exploited. Children came to school not infrequently from non-English speaking homes, as well as homes where the parents were absent from twelve to fourteen hours each day, working in sweat shops and factories. School enrollments grew at an alarming rate, and the public schools would have been ruined had it not been for the heroic efforts of numerous school societies, such as the Pennsylvania Society for the Promotion of Public Schools, and labor organizations such as the National Trades Union and the Philadelphia Working Man's Party that worked closely with the Pennsylvania Society for the Promotion of Public Schools.

The European normal school became the first institution for the professional preparation of teachers in the United States. It was a humble but strong beginning for professional preparation, and in the middle of the nineteenth century few elements of schooling in this country could have been thought strong. Luckily, there was strength in the dissatisfaction of many leading schoolmen, who were yet inspired with the faith in education that had characterized the country (54). This faith was linked with a realistic recognition that a people could not be free and ignorant. "If a nation expects to be ignorant and free in a state of civilization," wrote Jefferson to Colonel Yancey, "it expects what never was and never will be." George Washington had solemnly underscored the same thought in his "Farewell Address." "Promote then," he had urged, "as an object of primary importance, Institutions for the general diffusion of knowledge. In proportion as the structure of a government gives force to public opinion, it is essential that public opinion should be enlightened" (10:29).

While there was no lack of faith or of realism, there was also no strong central government, no equivalent to the European Ministry of Education, able to carry out the will of the monarch. If there were to be advances in formal education, Americans would have to press for them in their communities. And press they did. The Parent-Teacher Associations and the Citizens Committees for Public Education of the twentieth century are the successors to the friends of education in the nineteenth.

Prior to 1850, and for years thereafter, the greater number of teachers were young, unskilled, and poorly educated. In the Jacksonian era, they taught handicapped by spoils system as were the cities, but in the country teachers were not superior to their colleagues in the cities. Washington Irving's cruel satirization of Ichabod Crane in the *Legend of Sleepy Hollow*, (1810-1820) drew a stereotype of the country teacher in the early nineteenth century. School examiners in 1839 reported that in Ohio there was a prodigal waste of "money, intellect, and morals" occasioned by the employment of unqualified teachers. All too many New Jersey teachers were also counted incompetent, intemperate, and immoral. A pioneer in initiating the normal school for the professional preparation of teachers, James C. Carter, in 1824 described the teachers he had observed in New England primary grades as too young, too little wedded to teaching, and ". . . teachers who never had any direct preparation for their profession" (33:403).

These reports were sufficiently dismal to cause alarm. Belief in the importance of education had been voiced by every American political leader of the eighteenth and nineteenth centuries, and yet the American common school was described as a failure. The only way to turn was towards Europe, and quite a few laymen and state school officers went abroad in the 1840's and 1850's for the purpose of studying elementary schools, and above all, the Pestalozzian teacher-training schools, which had come to be called "normal schools" in France. The name meant only that in these schools teachers learned the principles of teaching. Though he was but one of these visitors, Horace Mann, secretary to the new State Board of Education in Massachusetts, was most successful in winning an interested audience with his reports, appearing annually between 1837 and 1848. The Seventh Annual Report (1843) treated most approvingly the Prussian elementary schools, many of whose teachers had been trained in Pestalozzian theory and techniques.

The first public normal school was opened in Massachusetts in 1839 by James C. Carter, some sixteen years after the Reverend Samuel R. Hall (1795-1877) had started one privately in his home at Concord, Vermont. Carter, who challenged Massachusetts in his advocacy of public provision for teacher-training, himself had had some ten years of experience in conducting a private normal school. Neither Carter nor Hall was unaware of what the academies were doing, but they understood that it was not enough simply to append to the so-called English course of the academy rudimentary instruction in how to teach and maintain discipline. The academies were just not prepared to cope with the demand for teachers.

In Europe, writings on education and on teaching were not wanting. But in Colonial America, and in the United States for the first half of the nineteenth century, there was a critical shortage of books on the effective management of a classroom. Samuel R. Hall's *Lectures in School-Keeping* (1829) was a landmark and an immediate success. The *Lectures* were eminently useful; nothing like them existed, and their utility was proven by the demand for copies. Published in 1829—the first book on education printed in the United States in the English language—every copy of its first edition was sold in two weeks. There is little reason to doubt the estimate of Wright and Gardner that the *Lectures* made a "practically inestimable contribution" to the advancement of professional preparation of teachers in the United States (62:20).

The inspiration for his lectures was his normal school, run on Pestalozzian principles. His classroom was equipped with a blackboard, perhaps the first in the United States (62:19-20), in order that students be practiced in illustrating objects about which they would teach. This was but a sign of the sense-realism characteristic of pedagogical theory after the initial mention of the blackboard by Comenius in his *Orbis pictus* (1658). All but four of the thirteen lectures comprising Hall's little book were practical, offering instruction on "the responsibility of the teacher," "the importance of gaining the confidence of the school," "the manner of treating scholars—uniformity in government—firmness . . . partiality . . . punishments—rewards," "modes of teaching—manner of illustrating subjects," "means of exciting the attention of scholars," and "methods of teaching spelling, reading, arithmetic, geography, English grammar, writing, history, and composition" (61).

Hall was followed by David P. Page, Principal of the State Normal School in Albany, New York, with the first of what would become a great flow of books in the United States on methods of teaching, counseling, and administering education. Twenty-four years had elapsed between the marketing of Hall's *Lectures* and Page's *Theory and Practice of Teaching.* In that generation, the state normal school had evolved. The preparation of school teachers in the techniques of teaching and in the subject-matter to be taught had begun in earnest. In contrast with Hall's *Lectures*, Page's *Theory and Practice of Teaching* acquainted its readers with a wide variety of instructional materials and a good deal of speculation on the powers of the child's mind. There were unmistakable signs of Page's acquaintance with European writings, certainly with those of Pestalozzi and Rousseau. Frequent references were made to an "appropriate," a "natural" order to be followed in introducing skills and subjects. "There is a natural order in the education of the child," he assured teachers, and it was one in which the "elements" of any study are taught and learned before complexity was introduced (46:21). Recognizing that a child must learn to crawl before he can be expected to start to walk, Page wrote that ". . . writing with a pen may well be deferred till the child is *ten years of age,* when the muscles shall have acquired sufficient strength to grasp and guide it" (46:23).

Theory and Practice of Teaching was a more complete treatise than Hall's, and a more sophisticated study of pedagogical theory and science was on the horizon. Emerson E. White's *The Elements of Pedagogy* (1886) was more than a halfway house for Americans. European writing on educational theory was far more sophisticated, and it would be the twentieth century before American thinkers were on the same level; but forward movement was appreciable well before 1900. White's *Elements* showed the author to be quite at home with the writings of European educational theorists. He was not unaware that a science of pedagogy was emerging in Europe to complement the philosophy of education, and it was this educational science, White predicted, that offered hope of progress (60:87). Though White did not understand by the "scientific study of children" what that study shortly was to become, he did employ the phrase. The Preface to his *Elements of Pedagogy* pointed to the ascendancy of the scientific study of pedagogy, and all White's practical suggestions on how to teach were derived from a scientific exposition of physical processes. This was the first exhibit of the new order of students of education.

Although White thought of his *Elements of Pedagogy* as a scientific treatise, the book barely missed being part of the vanguard of the new pedagogical science. Perhaps the clue to White's failure to be up with the times was that the *Elements* (and his *School Management* of 1893) omitted reference to Herbart. For twenty years, Herbartian thought had been the scientific and philosophic yeast in the European educational ferment. Word of this had almost reached the United States, but White had not heard it.

Perhaps the year that marked the next step in the American evolution of a sophisticated theory of teaching was 1892, the year of the publication of Charles A. McMurry's *The Elements of General Method* (based on the Principles of Herbart). Five years later, when the National Herbart Society was strong, Charles McMurry and his brother, Frank, published *The Method of the Recitation*. Not the least interesting fact about the 1897 publication was the note under Frank McMurry's name on the title page: "Professor of Pedagogics and Dean of Faculty of Teachers' College, University of Buffalo, N. Y." The professional preparation of teachers had arrived; it had won a place among the professional colleges of a university.

It was the dual appeal of Herbartian science of pedagogics—with Herbart's stress on moral development as the supreme end of education—and the approval of outstanding university professors that had carried the day for the professional program in teacher preparation. Many thought that a science of teaching had at last been born, and that schools no longer had to risk the uncertain skill of amateurs. With Herbartian principles at their command, teachers were thought to be possessed of "universal principles of method in learning, based not upon the whim of the teacher, but upon the common law of mental action which is universal with all children and students" (39:8). Linked with this science was assurance that "the Herbartians have the hardihood, in this age of moral skeptics, to believe not only in moral example but also in moral teaching. . . ." All but Darwinian naturalists were pleased.

The Herbartian method of teaching was the famous method of recitation. Of course, enlightened Herbartians, such as the McMurry brothers, Charles De Garmo, and William C. Bagley, insisted that recitation never be a parrot-like regurgitation. The mine-run of teachers, however, persisted in asking all the questions; they taught and questioned, and students learned and recited. At best, the Herbartian influence improved the organization of teaching; detailed lesson-planning and careful presentation of new material certainly was stressed. The lesson plans of teachers were to include key or leading questions, all types of devices for winning and holding attention of pupils, and techniques of giving assignments. The value of this careful preparation, however, is to be balanced against the fact that the teacher was not to deviate from the plan or to permit departure from it by the students. Even the amount of ground to be covered in an appointed day was spelled out. There was no flexibility, no room for imagination on the part of teacher or pupil, no adjustment to individual differences in the student body (53:11-12).

EVOLUTION OF THE NORMAL SCHOOL

Between 1820 to 1865 it had been decided, in the United States and in Europe, that teachers required special, professional preparation in addition to academic study. The type of preparation for elementary school teachers became distinguished from that of high school teachers. As in Europe, the first step in the preparation of high school teachers was attendance at a liberal arts college. The normal school, in this county and in Europe, for some time was dedicated only to the preparation of elementary school teachers.

It was realistic, as Borrowman (5) has explained, to feel as did Horace Mann in the 1840's, that the Prussian, Pestalozzian normal schools were adequate models for Americans. It was realistic, also, to propose that normal school students who were to teach in elementary schools study the subjects they were to teach; their grounding in the three R's, spelling, grammar, and geography could not be taken for granted. Many who entered normal school had not had more than two years of high school, nor did all who became elementary school teachers review their elementary school training and complete high school while studying in normal schools. For a quarter of a century after Appomattox, little enough was required in the way of professional preparation. The popular two-year normal school course offered a hodgepodge of English grammar, elementary arithmetic, writing, and drawing, the bare elements of geography, botany, physiology, chemistry, theory and practice of teaching, ethics, bookkeeping, algebra, United States history, and fragments of other subjects. What was demanded of the normal school graduate was that he be able to spell, write legibly, enunciate distinctly, solve arithmetic problems only up to percentages, and know the basic facts of United States geography and history. Good character and health always were demanded. By 1895, most elementary school teachers had less than a high school education, and as late as 1922 at least twenty-five per cent of elementary school teachers had not completed high school. Elementary schools and their staffs, whether in Europe or in the United States, always contrasted vividly with the staffs of secondary schools. In 1904, sixty per cent of the high school teachers in the United States had completed college, while at least half of the elementary school teachers had not completed a full high school course.

Right or wrong, the existence of the normal school was an admission that elementary school teachers were ill-educated. Unhappily, the normal school program of review of the elementary school subjects to be taught stigmatized teachers. They were not thought to have learned much beyond what their pupils would learn. Their critics gave them scant credit for what they learned of classroom management.

A second consequence of the distinction between the preparation of elementary and high school teachers was no less unfortunate. The normal school, in Europe as well as America, was labelled nonacademic. Professors at American colleges and European universities became outspokenly contemptuous of normal schools. When the latter introduced instruction in scientific methods of teaching, the academicians went on record as humanists who did not believe that education could be imparted scientifically, only nurtured by educated men and women. In order that teachers be educated, the humanists argued, they must attend colleges and universities and study liberal arts and sciences. The gulf between the preparation of elementary and secondary school teachers became a part of the chasm between collegiate faculties and those engaged in the professional preparation of teachers.

The debate between the two groups lay in the future; meanwhile the normal schools flourished, their number increasing almost seven hundred per cent between 1865 and 1895. With this expansion, normal schools also expanded their course of study, adding science subjects (even laboratory science in a few instances) and courses that were thought to include scientific study of the human mind and its processes (5:103-105). The Worcester, Massachusetts, normal school, encouraged by G. Stanley Hall, even had its students observing children rather than limiting themselves to reading about them.

THE TRANSFORMATION OF THE NORMAL SCHOOL

In Europe, it was not until the close of World War II that significant moves were made to improve the preparation of elementary school teachers and thus enhance their status. In the United States, many of the one- and two-year normal schools were transformed into teachers colleges before 1900; the trend had begun that would end only when the normal school had metamorphosed from state normal school, to state college, to professional school in a state university, a college of education charged with the professional preparation of teachers. In 1897, the Michigan legislature designated the normal school at Ypsilanti the Michigan State Normal School. Ypsilanti provided the first exhibition of this remarkable metamorphosis. By 1920, forty-six normal schools had evolved into state colleges (58: Chap. 16).

A DEVELOPMENT OF GREAT SIGNIFICANCE:
PROFESSIONAL ORGANIZATION

Concurrent with the growth of normal schools, of the idea that those who teach must be technically prepared, was the emergence of the National Teachers Association (1857). Medieval universities, following the lead of the craft guilds, had shown the utility of teacher organizations, not only for protection but for the maintenance of standards, at least in the courses of study that would lead to academic degrees. Teachers in the lower schools had for centuries followed the lead of the masters, but in the United States the first such venture was the National Teachers Association, which became the National Education Association of the United States in 1870 (58:44-45).

Never a union, the Association throughout its history has focused its effects far less on working conditions of teachers and administrators than on quality of curriculum and instruction. Though it is impossible to assess accurately influences on schools in Canada and the United States, doubtless it is true that in both countries, where professional organizations have been strong, neither state nor provincial bureaucracies, teachers colleges nor university departments of education, have had more to do with shaping the schools than the great professional bodies, with their special divisions devoted to the improvement of every subject matter field, as well as all phases of school organization and administration. Surely this holds true for the United States, where a traditional, Jeffersonian fear of strong central government vested the educational agency of the federal government and the United States Office of Education with virtually no authority over the nation's schools, except in areas of vocational education, schools for Indians and other dependents of the federal government, and, of course, schools serving the military establishments. Working together, the provincial and state departments of education, the teacher-training institutions, and the professional organizations have provided the national centralization of educational leadership found abroad.

Although the development of professional organizations can be dated from the inception of the National Teachers Association in 1857, there had been other important groups at work as early as 1826, when The American Lyceum was launched by Josiah Holbrook. The Lyceum had one overriding purpose, the improvement of the "common school," and it worked in all parts of the country, usually led by professional educators who told their audiences of the need for public schools, adequate teacher training, schooling for females, and schools free of sectarian and political control. The Lyceum did a very great deal with completely voluntary support of public-spirited men and women.

The Western Literary Institute, organized by Albert Picket in 1829, nevertheless while not as important as the Lyceum, accomplished much, particularly in the Southern and Midwestern states. That it did have influence might be surmised from the well-known educators who joined it. Its members included Calvin E. Stowe, W. H. McGuffey, Alexander Bache, and both Lyman and H. W. Beecher.

The New England counterpart of the Western Literary Institute was the American Institute of Instruction, active after 1830 and strong because of the participation of James G. Carter, George B. Emerson, Horace Mann, Leverett Saltonstall, and Henry Barnard, certainly among the most distinguished friends of education in New England.

These institutes, wherever they were located, devoted their discussions, public and private, and their publications to questions of the best subjects to teach and how they should be taught. The way was thus paved for large-scale, professional discussion of these topics.

Perhaps the institutes were rather less concerned with the elementary school and with students who would not continue their schooling beyond high school. The plight of teachers also was not a favored topic. In 1849, the American Association for the Advancement of Education was formed, and announced its intention to draw public attention to the problems of the lower schools. Horace Mann became the Association's first president, with Henry Barnard chairman of the business committee. The Association, whose life was but ten years, was the last of the informal, voluntary associations for the advancement of public education in the United States prior to the appearance in 1857 of the National Teachers' Association, later to become the National Education Association.

While none of the earlier groups had centered its attention on the lot of teachers, the National Teachers' Association advertised itself as dedicated to insuring teachers "the dignity, respectability, and usefulness of their calling." Of all the professional education organizations, the National Educational Association and the several Canadian education associations have been the most influential in lifting the sights of teachers and administrators. There have been other associations and professional societies devoted to special fields, such as the American Personnel and Guidance Association, or to fostering studies in the broad field of education, such as the National Society for the Study of Education, the Progressive Education Society, the John Dewey Society, and others; but the National Education Association has loomed largest, extending its influence steadily after 1880.

Not till 1960 did the United States Office of Education begin to offer leadership even slightly approximating that of the professional associations.

In the United States toward the close of the last century, the National Education Association very nearly remade elementary and secondary school courses in a series of most influential committees and commissions. It sponsored "one of the truly remarkable reports in the history of American education, that of the Committee of Ten on Secondary School Studies [45], published in 1893" (58:296). At about the same time, elementary education was addressed by the National Education Association's Department of Superintendence, which created the Committee of Fifteen for the study of elementary schooling (44). This Committee, it should be remarked, was headed by no less than the United States Commissioner of Education, the internationally known philosopher and superintendent of schools, William Torrey Harris.

The Committee of Ten on Secondary School Studies, the Committee of Fifteen on Elementary Education, the Committee on College Entrance Requirements, and the many committees and commissions that succeeded these (57:Chap. 25) illustrated what voluntary groups of professional educators could do without the direction of a federal education agency in the United States.

Further advances toward a profession. For centuries, teachers had been licensed in Europe, at first under the auspices of the bishops of the Roman Catholic Church, then by town and city officials, and finally by national ministries of education. In the United States all professional licensing, whether of physicians or of teachers, evolved much more slowly from apprenticeship. During the first half of the nineteenth century, local school authorities examined applicants for teaching posts and granted teaching certificates. A Massachusetts law of 1826 required the members of the school committee of each town to satisfy themselves by personal examination "of every teacher's literary qualifications and capacity for government of the school" (48:65).

New England states, with Vermont in the lead, moved toward centralizing licensing. A Vermont law of 1845 created the office of County Superintendent, among whose duties was the examination of candidates for teaching. A successful applicant was granted a certificate of approval, valid for one year.

By the middle of the century there was sufficient discussion of European practice and of the weaknesses in the schools of the United States to make educated people conscious of the genuine need for betterment of the teaching staffs. Nevertheless, until 1907 there was not even one state that required graduation from high school for certification! The state of Indiana introduced the requirement. But standards for certification gradually were raised, noticeably so after 1910. More professional study of child growth

119

and development, tests and measurements, and methods of teaching were required. By 1911, thirty-four states had minimal requirements for professional study.

While there had been movement toward more meaningful standards of certification, requirements for entry into the profession were not high. In 1926, only four states asked that teachers have two years of schooling beyond high school; fifteen states had no definite scholastic requirement. In the next thirty years, however, requirements for entry were genuinely strengthened, especially for elementary school teachers. A most promising move was made in 1946, with the initiation by the National Education Association of a National Commission on Teacher Education and Professional Standards (TEPS). The national TEPS commission and the TEPS commissions within the individual states stated as goals:

> . . . discriminating selection of those admitted to teacher preparation, and adjusted supply of qualified teachers, through preparation of teachers, certification requirements of four college years for beginning and five years for fully qualified teachers, continuous professional growth of teachers in service, professional accreditation of all teacher-training institutions, a professional concept of teaching, and adequate provision for teacher welfare (58:351).

BIBLIOGRAPHY

See the references at the end of Chapter 11.

In 1909, educators had occasion to observe the first trial of a unique institution designed for the early years of adolescence when the American junior high school made its debut in Berkeley, California. Superintendent Frank F. Bunker of Berkeley was one of the first advocates of a three-year school, intermediate between a senior high school and a six-year elementary school. As early as 1880 (58:78) voices have been heard urging the economizing of time in the elementary schools. This economy was to be achieved by introducing after the sixth grade subjects normally reserved for the first year of the American four-year high school. Another factor added force to the proposal for an intermediate stage between elementary and secondary education. Educators dissatisfied with the generally unimaginative curriculum and routine of high school teaching hoped that a new, three-year school would offer an opportunity to experiment. The 6-3-3 organization of education in the United States won popularity from the beginning. In the first year of its

121

EDUCATION IN THE RECENT PAST:
Reorganization of Elementary and Secondary Schools

10

trial, eleven junior high schools were opened; in ten years there were 880, and by 1954 the United States counted 3,227 (58:78) with enrollment well in excess of a million-and-a-half.

During the 1950's, a great deal was written and said in the United States and Canada on behalf of greater opportunities for the gifted and academically talented student (52). To some, it appeared as though these students had been discovered for the first time, and that their potentiality as a human resource, to be exploited for the advantage of society and for their own personal development, had gone unnoticed in other years. Of course, this was not the case. Those labelled "genius" indeed had suffered from a mistaken notion that their genius was coupled with a proneness to insanity (52:24-25). In 1891, one of the early studies of genius (Sir Francis Galton's *Hereditary Genius* had been published in 1869), Lombroso's *Men of Genius*, linked greatness with insanity. Nesbit's *The Insanity of Genius* only reinforced Lombroso's case, and a stereotype of the emotionally unstable man of genius rapidly took hold on men's imaginations. It is impossible to know what handicaps to unusual ability this stereotype created. Happily it appeared not to restrain schoolmen in the United States in their efforts to provide for students who achieved in a superior fashion.

122

The first undertaking on behalf of the most successful students, *defined in terms of performance in academic subjects*, had been to hurry them through the grades. In 1868, St. Louis had "flexible promotions" which permitted those who learned rapidly to finish the eight-year elementary school in six or seven years, without skipping any essentials in the subject-matter sequence. In 1886, schools in Elizabeth, New Jersey, innovated "sectioning," or grouping students by academic performance. Around 1900, Stuyvesant High School opened in New York City for boys of superior ability in mathematics, science, and the mechanic arts.

In 1895, when Preston W. Search, Superintendent of Schools in Los Angeles, read his paper, "Individualism in Mass Education," to the National Education Association's Department of Superintendence at its national meeting, he found himself well ahead of the thinking of most schoolmen. Although his audience did not approve his suggestion that there be attempts at individualizing instruction in order to recognize realistically differing levels of ability, one superintendent of schools, John Kennedy of Batavia, New York, certainly did respond to Search (40:101-110), introducing around 1898 periods of supervised study supplementing the regular recitations. By assigning two teachers to a single large class (of some sixty-five students), Kennedy made it possible for one teacher to offer the usual class instruction while the other helped the slow students and saw to it that the very rapid learners had supplementary materials. In a very real sense, the Batavia plan was the beginning of enrichment for the superior student and remediation for students with difficulties.

Search, whose address to the superintendents had been far from a success, had reason for confidence in the possibilities of moving towards individualization of instruction. What had drawn him to the attention of the school board of Los Angeles was his work in Pueblo, Colorado, where he had become superintendent in 1888. In those days, Pueblo was very much on the frontier; parents were not enthusiastic about academic accomplishment, and complained at the amount of homework assigned. Search abolished home study and initiated supervised study in school—a plan taken up by Kennedy in Batavia, and today a fixture in most American schools. The purpose of the Pueblo plan of supervised study, however, was not simply to relieve students of homework under conditions that made home study most difficult. Search knew that the conventional assignment-study-recitation routine simply did not make allowances either for the rapid learners or for those who could not make adequate progress without help. His plan highlighted individual students, whose individual needs had gone unattended in most schools for centuries. Even in the classrooms of the eighteenth and nineteenth centuries, when students often recited individually to the teacher rather than taking turns to recite while the whole class listened, the teacher was not *working* with the individual pupil and helping him to learn; the teacher was simply hearing recitations.

More influential than either the Pueblo or the Batavia plans was the teaching of Frederick L. Burke, assigned to the "training school department" of the San Francisco Teachers College. Teaching machines were years in the future when Burke, just prior to World War I, directed the preparation of self-teaching texts. On his staff was Carleton Washburne, who was to write one of the first studies of the "new education" in Europe (*New Schools in the Old World*, 1926) and become a guiding light in the progressive education movement in the United States. Differentiation in instruction took a long step forward while Washburne was superintendent of schools in Winnetka, Illinois, as it did under the guidance of Helen Parkhurst (*Education of the Dalton Plan*, 1922). The Dalton Plan, tried not only in the United States but also abroad, employed a contract system in which students, for part of the day, worked individually at tasks for which they had contracted. Clearly, the rapid learners would be able to move at their own pace, and since a portion of the day was spent in whole-class or group activities, the students would not lose the sense of being associated with others in the business of learning and living.

Those who learned with ease and were keen to learn were not overlooked during the first half of this century. Plan after plan, device after device was tried in their behalf, but few were adequately evaluated; the means of scientific evaluation were not available to the early experimenters. In the 1920's grouping on the basis of intelligence and accomplishment was all the rage, as acceleration had been twenty years previously. Then, in the 1930's, the term *enrichment* came into use; the work of the most able and eager students was to be enriched with supplementary learning, rather than having the student rushed through the grades in order that he might save a year or two. The attention to the able was genuine, and in 1920 the National Society for the Study of Education published as its nineteenth yearbook, *Classroom Problems in the Education of Gifted Children*.

Agitation for special provision for the education of the handicapped was noticeably minimal, at least in the United States. Voluntary groups of laymen, of parents, did not organize; perhaps parents of handicapped children were too ashamed to make their plight public. Only very recently has this tendency been reversed, and generations have passed with but a few compassionate and able men working to reduce the educational handicaps of blind, deaf or otherwise gravely burdened children.

A Spaniard, Juan Pablo Bonet (d. 1629), invented a manual alphabet for the deaf, published in Madrid in 1620. Jacob Rodrigues Pereire (1715-1780) hit upon the process of lip reading, by which any number of the deaf have been taught to speak and understand. For his discovery, Pereire was decorated by Louis XV, King of France (57:6), a fragment of evidence that the court of Versailles was not without humane sympathies.

By 1760, there was a special school for the deaf which had been opened by Thomas Braidwood in Edinburgh. But almost nothing had been done in the field by Americans until Thomas Gallaudet, who had observed the use of the sign alphabet in France and opened a school for the deaf in Hartford, Connecticut, in 1816. His experiment did not sufficiently impress the New England legislatures, however, and it was the state of Kentucky that established the first state school for the deaf in 1823.

France had a school for the blind as early as 1784, when Valentine Hatty taught children to read embossed books that he was able to have printed in Paris. In America, Boston and New York City had private schools for the blind by 1832, but the first American public school for the blind opened in Chicago in 1900.

It appears that the education of the handicapped, certainly of those handicapped by emotional and mental disorders, has been hindered by the rather primitive attitudes of laymen. The problems simply have not been squarely faced; handicaps have not been accepted as unfortunate accidents that a child or youth could be taught to adjust to, or in the instance of emotional disease, to overcome if the child and his family could be treated together. But professionals in the field of special education have accumulated knowledge, aided by findings in medicine, psychiatry, clinical psychology, social work, and sociology. Nor have professionals forgotten that their largest handicap is public and parental attitude.

World War II, however, found even more groups of parents with common problems banded together for joint appeal to state legislatures for funds to bolster studies in educating, as well as treating, handicapped youngsters. The problems had at least come into the open.

STANDARDIZATION

The call for individualization of instruction was answered only by the most imaginative and daring. A historian might be persuaded that in Europe and the United States the early demands for individualization were premature. The school systems, at least in the United States, had not been standardized to a degree permitting an observer in 1890 to predict the general pattern of schooling to be found in any portion of the country.

Individualization was a step that only a mature system of education might take. Educators would have to be sure of themselves, and schoolmen in the United States at the turn of the century were not sure of themselves. Who knew of what elementary or high school education should consist? There were any number of patterns. The setting of some standards by the powerful National Education Association committees reporting between 1890 and 1900 was a step toward standardization and maturity that very few have appreciated. If anything, these committees—the Committee of Ten on Secondary School Studies (45) and the Committee on College Entrance Requirements (43)—have been described as having most unfortunate consequences because they were dominated by faculties from colleges and universities that were presumed to be interested only in the academic training of the handful of high school students who would continue on to college. Even the Committee of Fifteen on Elementary Education (44) has been criticized for recommending an economizing of time in the elementary school in order to introduce high school subjects after the sixth grade. Children, it was said in criticism of the Committee's report, need time to grow up and must not be thought of simply as scholars; they have needs beyond that for encountering sooner high school studies. The Committee was also accused of forgetting other needs—for "socialization," learning to live comfortably and rewardingly with others, and so on.

These criticisms may well have been unjustified, in part if not totally. But their validity or invalidity is not the whole story here, although it is central to an accurate estimate of the National Education Association committees. On a par with the importance of resolving this issue in the record of the history of education in the United States is the import of the *constituency* of the committees. For on these committees, for the last time in half a century, the leaders of the American academic world—some of the most distinguished scholars and college administrators in the land—worked in close harmony with superintendents, principals, and a few classroom teachers. In 1905 Nicholas M. Butler, President of Columbia University, who was most interested in the advancement of public education and the preparation of teachers, withdrew from the National Education Association. It may be that he resented the addition of classroom teachers to the Association, but for whatever reason, his withdrawal signaled the disengagement of almost all the other academicians. Communication thus ended between these subject-matter specialists and those who taught in the elementary and high schools, as well as those who supervised the professional preparation of those teachers. The stage was set for the attacks by professors on the curriculum of the elementary and high schools and the teachers colleges—attacks that became so conspicuous in the debate on education that began when the Second World War ended.

The late Ellwood P. Cubberley, onetime dean of American historians of education, writing in his *Public Education in the United States*, described and judged the Committee of Ten on Secondary School Studies and its companion committees on college entrance requirements and the elementary school.

These committees were dominated by subject-matter specialists, possessed of a profound faith in the value of mental discipline. No study of pupil abilities, social needs, interest, capacities, or differential training found a place in their deliberations. The basis of their recommendations throughout was that of individual judgment. It was twenty years afterward before any use was made of grade placement and the organization of the materials of the curriculum. As the committees supported one another, their views became accepted and the reconstructed curriculum which followed became crystallized and difficult to change. There was much vigorous dissent from teachers, but for a long time it was not influential. A change came only as we turned from college presidents and professors, subject-matter specialists, and private school executives, whose interests were in mind training, scholarship as such, and knowledge for the knowledge's sake, and who compiled their reports by armchair philosophic methods, to students of education practices who applied experimental and quantitative method to the solution of educational problems and built their report on the result of experimental research (13:543-544).

Cubberley was justified in suggesting that the members of the committees did not know systematic psychology of child development—intellectual, social, and emotional—and that they were equally short on adolescent psychology. One must also grant that Cubberley was almost correct in saying "No study of differential training found a place in their deliberations" for *there were no studies of this type available.* The members of the committee were not deliberately ignoring the research of educational psychology; that research had yet to be produced. If they employed "individual judgment" and "armchair philosophic methods" rather than research techniques only recently available, they had no alternative. This was a loss, no doubt, but not one sufficient to cancel the excellence of their individual judgment.

Reading the reports of these committees cannot but convince one that the authors were reasonable men. They did not write as though they felt that the interests of children were of no concern. Of course, not all of them would have been open-minded when presented with the findings of psychologists at a later day, but in all probability most would have, acknowledging that teaching would be more effective when the motives, interests, and abilities of the learners had been taken into account.

THE COMMITTEE OF TEN ON SECONDARY SCHOOL STUDIES

The three major committees of the NEA in the 1890's were: the Committee of Ten on Secondary School Studies (42), the Committee of Fifteen on Elementary Education (44), and the Committee on College Entrance Requirements (43).

Of the three, the Committee of Ten on Secondary School Studies has been remembered best. President Eliot organized the committee most efficiently, appointing subcommittees to deal with separate school subjects. There were nine subcommittees, their titles suggesting the model American secondary school course in the late nineteenth century: (1) Latin, (2) Greek, (3) English, (4) Other Modern Languages, (5) Mathematics, (6) Physics, Astronomy, and Chemistry, (7) Natural History (Biology, including elements of Botany, Zoology, and Physiology), (8) History, Civil Government, and Political Economy, (9) Geography (Physical Geography and Ecology).

The reports of the conference groups made it plain that the members were only interested in making instruction effective. They did not try to build empires, urging that all students be required to study their subject, be it Latin, Greek, mathematics, or a modern foreign language. Although staffed largely by college professors, the groups were sensitive to the limitations of young minds and their need for instruction that would stimulate their curiosity rather than simply discipline their minds.

> The Mathematical Conference recommends that the course in arithmetic in elementary school be abridged, and recommends only a moderate assignment of time to algebra and geometry (45:14).

The abridgment of the course of study in arithmetic and mathematics was to result in ". . . omitting entirely those subjects which perplex and exhaust the pupil without affording any really valuable mental discipline enriched by a greater number of exercises in simple calculation and in the solution of concrete problems" (45:105). This was a modern recommendation. The term "enrichment" has become a current coin.

One must read at even greater length from the Mathematical Conference report because its sane and humane attitude was characteristic of each of the conference groups. Each urged teachers to deal with interesting, commonplace ideas before moving to difficult, complex abstractions.

A stereotype, and quite a false one, existed, that scholars in the several fields of the liberal arts were convinced that secondary school education should consist in drill and the discipline of arduous study of subjects that need not be interesting to the student. This stereotype did not hold for the Mathematical Conference of the Committee of Ten and its chairman, Simon Newcomb, a distinguished mathematician and a professor of mathematics at Johns Hopkins University. Nor did it hold for the English Conference, whose chairman was George Lyman Kittredge of Harvard, a renowned Shakespearean scholar. His groups did not recommend that the study of English be a matter of drill, of parsing sentences, syntax, and grammar. The very first sentence of the English Conference's report reads:

> The main direct objects of the teaching of English in schools seem to be two: (1) to enable the pupil to understand the expressed thoughts of others and to give expression to thoughts of his own; and (2) to cultivate a taste for reading, to give the pupil some acquaintance with good literature, and to furnish him with the means of extending that acquaintance (45:86).

In its report, furthermore, the English subcommittee recommended that grammar be allotted *no more than an hour a week in the fourth year* (for a total of forty hours) *of high school* (45:91).

For high school, the Committee of Ten drew up a list of some eleven questions on which the groups were to report. These could be reduced to three broad questions: (1) What are appropriate courses for the secondary schools and how best may they be taught? (2) What distinction, if any, shall be made in teaching students who will continue on to college and those who will not? (3) What constitutes appropriate requirements for admission to college? Neither the original eleven nor the three to which they were reduced would be adequate for the guidance of schools today. They did not grapple with the place of vocational training in the secondary school (16). The Committee felt that the most pressing questions concerned how to improve the quality of courses being offered in secondary school so that they would be useful both to young people who would not go on to college and to those who would.

The effects of the Committee of Ten and the Committee on College Entrance Requirements. The Committee of Ten and the Committee on College Entrance Requirements did have the effect of standardizing the *college preparatory course of study* in the American high school. Some historians have felt that this was unfortunate. To them, as to Cubberley, it meant that the secondary school was seen as nothing but a college-preparatory school, and under the dominance of colleges whose staffs were not interested in any but the small fraction of youth who would be coming to college.

These historians have missed the point. As a result of the NEA committee work, the college entrance course of study was systematized, standardized, and improved, hence it *was* the superior course of study in the secondary school. *What was needed was not a weakening of that program but a similar study of alternative programs designed for students other than those whose educational future lay with the liberal arts college.* In a word, American secondary schools needed another course in addition to the college-preparatory course; at the time, there was no such course.

Historians have given much more attention to the Committee of Ten on Secondary Studies than they have to the Committee of Fifteen on Elementary Education. This was not due to any failure of the Committee of Fifteen to publish a significant report; rather it was the imbalance in attention occasioned by the fact that in the twentieth century the controversies about education were most sharp on the question of whether secondary education should be chiefly college-preparatory.

The Committee of Fifteen did not deserve to be overlooked; it embodied a subcommittee report which recommended the *systematic professional preparation of teachers*. This recommendation had not been spelled out so well before, nor had it carried so much weight. Ignoring the other two subcommittees of the Committee of Fifteen—on the Organization of City School Systems and The Correlation of Studies in the Elementary School —the subcommittee on Training of Teachers lent prestige to the idea that teachers must be educated beyond academic subjects. In the first pages of the subcommittee report it was clearly stated that "Professional study differs widely from academic study." For the future teacher there must be a study of children. "Most fundamental and important of the professional studies which ought to be pursued by one intending to teach is psychology" (44:24). The subcommittee foresaw the need for a scientific study of behavior and the process of learning if teaching was to be improved. This was well in advance of a movement for the scientific study of education.

129

> Modern educational thought emphasizes the opinion that the child, not the subject of study, is the guide to the teacher's efforts. To know the child is of paramount importance. How to know the child must be an important item of instruction to the teacher in training. The child must be studied as to his physical, mental, and moral condition. Is he in good health? Are his senses of sight and hearing normal, or in what degree abnormal? . . . What are his likes and dislikes? . . . By what tests can

the degree of difference between bright and dull children be estimated?
(44:24-25)

Despite the standardization intended by the National Education Association committees, the new century witnessed a proliferation of separate school studies in the elementary and high schools. The seven elementary school subjects of the 1880's—spelling, reading, writing, arithmetic, geography, grammar, and United States history—had become a dozen by 1900.

> By 1930 the typical school in cities offered eighteen and by 1950 the number had grown to about thirty. An even more rapid growth of subjects occurred in the high school. A committee report of 1891 lists about thirty subjects. Modern and American history were conspicuously absent. In 1923 a superintendent reported that one large city high school listed 168 subjects. At the normal rate of progress it would, he said, take a student fourteen years to take all of them. By the 1950's the offerings were about as broad as human knowledge, but by the latter date no one tried to limit offerings to the capacities of one student. Thus the concept of an overcrowded curriculum was a reflection of social progress and not the assignment for any one pupil (58:111).

Joined with the swelling of the program of studies was a rapid enlargement of the student body in both American elementary and high schools, most visibly in the high schools. In 1890, there were 2526 high schools in the United States with an elrollment of 359,949 students. This increased to almost 700,000 within ten years, and almost doubled again in each succeeding decade till 1940 (58:60). A similar rate of growth in academic schooling did not occur in Europe, where a much smaller percentage of elementary school graduates expected, or were expected, to enter secondary school, at least academic or nonvocational secondary school.

The National Education Association committees of the 1890's had set the precedent for review of the curriculum by the profession. In accord with this precedent, the Association set up its Commission on the Reorganization of Secondary Education in 1913. No other committee or commission in this country's educational history has had an effect comparable with that of the Commission on Reorganization (41).

> This large Commission, operating through sixteen subcommittees, utilized the services of hundreds of public-school men and a few college professors. Between 1913 and 1921 it issued thirteen reports on such topics as civics, social studies, English, music, physical education, moral values, and guidance, which had a distribution of over 200,000. . . . In 1918 appeared its epoch-making report on *Cardinal Principles of Secondary Education*. Probably no publication in the history of education ever surpassed this little five-cent, thirty-two-page booklet in importance, both because of its fundamental nature and because of its influence.
> Unlike the Committee of Ten and previous committees, the Commission on Reorganization started by examining the environmental influences

that called for changes in education. Reorganization was needed because society had changed; because the student body had increased enormously, this increasing the range of needs and abilities; because education theory had brought new knowledge and new interpretations. Conscious of the social setting, the needs of student, the nature of learning, and the fitness of curricular materials, the Commission proclaimed the seven cardinal objectives or purposes: health, basic skills, home membership, vocations, citizenship, worthy use of leisure, and character. Student-oriented, life-centered, and socially-directed, these purposes marked a sharp departure from the old college-preparatory studies (58:75-76).

Wesley's concluding comment on the 1918 report, the *Cardinal Principles of Secondary Education,* itself was revealing of things to come. Such phrases as "student-oriented," "life-centered," and "socially directed," contrasted with such a phrase as "the old college-preparatory studies," bespoke a philosophy of education and became the labels and libels thrown about in the great debate on education that marked the decade from 1950 to 1960. The idea of orienting studies to the needs of youth, however imperfectly it was carried out, did give modern American education its peculiar quality. For one thing, attendance to the needs of youth—heightened by the serious plight of adolescents in the depression of the 1930's (3)—called into a more active role high school guidance and counseling services. Much more thought was given to the needs of youths who would not further their training beyond high school; thinking of them, Prosser, Director of the Dunwoody (Vocational) Institute in Minneapolis, coined his famous, or infamous, phrase "life-adjustment education"—education for the sixty per cent of the youths who, before the Second World War, would not attend school after their high school graduation, or after they had reached the age at which they could legally leave school.

From experts on the curriculum one heard much about the need for a core or a general education that would be available to all students faced with the great number of elective courses that had been invented by 1940. It was this desire for a core of studies, for a general education, that bore fruit in such expressions as the "common learnings" (used in the 1944 report of the Educational Policies Commission, *Education for All American Youth*) (16), or after 1944, in such words as "the core curriculum." American educators went all out for general education, and they had their critics who feared that "general science" would be watered down physics, chemistry and biology; after all, general social studies appeared to be less rigorous geography and history. The criticism was loudest when the general education movement promised, or threatened, to reach the college (as it did with the endorsement of a special committee of Harvard College, reporting, in 1945, in *General Education in a Free Society.*

BIBLIOGRAPHY

See the references at the end of Chapter 11.

At the time that elementary and high school curriculums underwent fundamental as well as extensive alteration, the American college did not go untouched. It had escaped change for a remarkably long time; for some two hundred years it had retained its British pattern without fundamental modification (7:96). The European universities were equally stable, only adding to the traditional arts faculties (and those of medicine, law, and theology) the new faculty of social science in the twentieth century. The American collegiate mold was broken after the Civil War by three events: the passage of the Morrill Land Grant Act (1862), the expansion of the course of study by the innovation of an elective system, and the importation of the graduate school from Germany. In these years, too, the American college became standardized as a four-year institution, granting a bachelor's degree.

THE MORRILL LAND GRANT ACT OF 1862

The Morrill Act established public, low-tuition colleges, thus opening

AMERICAN
HIGHER
EDUCATION
IN TRANSITION

11

the doors of higher education to young men and women who could not afford the tuitions of private colleges. Further, the Act was partially successful in making mechanical arts and agriculture respectable studies in advanced education. To this day there are those who refer to the state universities, which, for the most part, developed as a result of the Act, as "cow colleges." These "cow colleges" revolutionized American agriculture, and provided the foundation for several of the finest schools of engineering sciences.

Less earth-shaking was the victory won by those who wanted to broaden the collegiate course of study and permit students to exercise choice in the selection of courses (7:Chap. 6). If one name only were to be remembered in connection with electives, it would be that of Charles William Eliot, President of Harvard from 1869 to 1909. Eliot championed the idea of election and won. His argument, that had to be carried against the classical humanists, drew on the example of the European university where students were free to elect their own studies, even wandering from university to university to study with professors whose reputation attracted them. Eliot met strong opposition but overcame it. For the most part, objections to an elective system charged that students would not receive a general education including the essentials that should be the possessions of any truly educated man (7:109).

133

The victory of the elective system simply postponed the day when colleges would again have to face the rhetorical question: What constitutes a liberal or general education, to which all college graduates should be exposed in addition to any specialization in a field, or any spread of elected courses? In the years that followed Eliot's tenure at Harvard, no other question would so deeply trouble the staffs of American colleges and universities. It was not strange that a similar question was not heard in Europe, where a general education was to be provided by the secondary school. Specialization at the European university was taken for granted.

In more than one great American college, there were experiments to overcome the narrow specialization that so often resulted from free election (7:265). New interdisciplinary courses and sequences of courses were announced at Columbia and Dartmouth. Alexander Meikeljohn persuaded the University of Wisconsin to try a new, two-year experimental college (7:266). Meikeljohn's ambition was to devote the first year to a study in depth of ancient Greek and Roman civilization. The second year was to study modern civilization, perhaps American, after the same fashion. "The main aim would be not so much to gain information, although that was important, as to develop a philosophical habit of mind in grasping the over-all significance of the way the various parts of a culture interact" (7:266).

Meikeljohn's experiment touched off others, principally the two-year college at the University of Chicago inaugurated by Robert M. Hutchins. The great books curriculum, based on classics in several fields, was St. John's College's (Maryland) venture in general education. There were other trials at providing undergraduate two-year general education, one of the most successful at the University of Minnesota.

The definition of a liberal or general education never was made in a universally acceptable fashion. The pressures for specialized undergraduate programs mounted, and research-oriented graduate schools for the preparation of specialists grew increasingly stronger.

GRADUATE AND PROFESSIONAL SCHOOLS IN THE UNITED STATES

The university had arisen to train men in the "learned professions" of law, medicine, and theology. Not till the nineteenth century, however, was there a willing acknowledgment that learning in all fields might be advanced by research in libraries and laboratories, which, by and large, was only available in universities. This vision of expanding the reach of knowledge by scholars in universities quickly had added to it the idea that the process of discovery would die with the generation unless a new group of scholars were trained. Apprenticeship was the best-known and most handy method of rearing a new generation of scholars; graduate education was simply the latest development in apprenticeship training.

Inadequate as they were, the normal schools for teachers were among the very few professional schools in the country. Apprenticeship had become the sole manner of training physicians, lawyers, and Protestant ministers. True, neither Catholic priests nor Jewish rabbis lacked formal schooling in their theology and religion, but the Protestant clergy in the United States seems to have had special problems in financing "professional" ministerial schooling. "The professional candidate placed himself under an able and mature minister, lawyer, or doctor and hoped by observation and imitation to be admitted subsequently to professional status" (7:196). All in all, the apprenticeship period of professional preparation lacked both rigor and thoroughness.

The one profession that in the early years of this nation appeared likely to receive collegiate attention was law. Law made its bow in the United States as a professional study shortly after the Revolutionary War, when Thomas Jefferson inaugurated a professorship in legal studies at the College of William and Mary (7:198). Not till almost forty years later did faculties of theology appear at Harvard and Yale.

By the beginning of the nineteenth century, enterprising men had opened a few private professional training schools which operated, hopefully, for a profit. A group of physicians might join together to form a school for physicians. "Some successful pastors were accepting not just one, or even two, but a number of young men to study with them for the ministry. Although not formally organized as schools, these aggregations were widely known as 'schools of the prophets' " (7:199). These proprietary schools were popular complements of the apprenticeship system, but they lacked entrance requirements, rigorous examinations, and, as might be guessed, instruction of high quality (7:204).

As with the elective system, it was President Eliot who took the risk of raising the standards of admission to the professional training programs at Harvard. Enrollments did fall, as the critics had forecast, but the drop was temporary (7:202-203). Once admission standards were raised, the revision of the curriculum soon followed. Teaching methods also benefited, in turn.

Medical education was slated for the most thoroughgoing renovation. A report of Abraham Flexner, published in 1910, marks the point at which professional medical education in the United States and Canada entered a period of excellence. Supported by the Carnegie Foundation for the Advancement of Teaching, Flexner's study of medical education "produced a veritable revolution in medical education" (7:205). Medical schools had been graded A, B, or C by the American Medical Association, but in light of Flexner's report on the weakness of most medical education, this classification had meant but little. Flexner's exposé had remarkable effects. By 1930, only three medical schools remained in class B and six in class C (7:206).

The lightning that struck medical education spared the other professions for a generation, but no one of them went for this period without some review by its members. By 1960, all professions had evaluated themselves, not once but several times. They emerged strengthened, only to find that their new higher standards of admission and training, their joining hands with graduate schools preoccupied with research and the advancement of learning, demanded enormous quantities of money? While the private foundations had the habit of generous giving, the question was written large; must higher education, undergraduate as well as graduate, in private or state institutions, openly turn to the federal government and its agencies for regular, large-scale support? In Europe, this question was not raised because the universities were supported by the national treasuries or by municipalities; the private university was all but unknown.

The question of how far to depend upon federal grants became one of the issues of great moment for higher education in the 1960's. Attempts to police the patriotism and the religious, political, economic, and intellectual orthodoxy of the administrators and professors would have been back had the colleges and universities not been made wary. In the United States, the professor or administrator was not as invulnerable as his counterpart had become in Europe.

THE JUNIOR COLLEGE

Closely related to the anxieties of financing higher education was the certainty that demands for education beyond high school in the United States would create new colleges, as they have done.

The junior college was one response to the popular appeal for education beyond high school. Though a relatively recent addition to higher education, the junior college has proved itself to be one of the most useful segments of advanced schooling in the United States. An American innovation, the first junior college opened in Joliet, Illinois, in 1902. In the 1920's, the junior college became an attractive institution in many communities where citizens desired post-high school education close to home (34, 37). Some fifty years after the first junior college, there were almost six hundred in the United States, with an enrollment in excess of six hundred thousand students. The junior college may well be the chief assistance to colleges and universities facing the growing demands for higher education.

ADVANCED EDUCATION FOR WOMEN

"American colleges," observed Schmidt, "like European universities, were for men. Harvard had been in existence for two hundred years before any serious attempts were made to provide the same kind of higher education for women" (50:124).

The need for educating women had been acknowledged in the United States early in its national life, but action on it was slow to come. When it was acknowledged, the recognition was not that women needed education for personal development, but that they required schooling beyond high school in order to be more interesting wives, and above all, good mothers. Schooling of women, in Noah Webster's words, "should . . . enable them to implant in the tender mind such sentiments of virtue, propriety, and dignity as are suited to the freedom of our government" (20:16).

Colleges for women grew out of the academies and seminaries, one of the first of which was the Moravian Academy for girls in Bethlehem, Pennsylvania. Receiving its first class in 1786, the Academy illustrated the high regard in which the Moravians, to whom Comenius had belonged, held education. In 1836, Mary Lyon announced that Mount Holyoke Seminary would welcome young ladies. In 1855, Elmira College in Elmira, New York, lent the title "college" to the education of women. In 1865, Vassar Female College opened with the endowment, magnificent for the day, of $800,000, "the gift of Matthew Vassar, English-born businessman of Poughkeepsie who had made a fortune brewing ale" (50:130). Wellesley and Smith Colleges came on the scene ten years later, and Bryn Mawr followed in 1885. It was in the higher education of women that one of the most promising steps in advanced education was taken in the later 1950's. Women who had completed college and sometimes professional school, only to have their careers cut short by marriage and rearing a family, were allowed to return to college or professional school either to have renewed or refurbished their technical and professional training, which they had dropped fifteen or more years earlier. It is this recognition on the part of schools of the needs of some women that is the latest step in the extension of educational opportunity.

In the larger field of adult education, the United States has far less to remark than England and the Scandinavian countries. However, it would seem that adult education should appear prominently in the history of education during the second half of the twentieth century.

IN CONCLUSION

The outlook for education during the remainder of the twentieth century is especially bright. Conditions for educational advances have never been so promising. Public support for generous financing of education seems assured because there is widespread realization that education is an investment that pays handsome dividends, both to the individuals educated and to society. There will be a continuing demand for greater educational opportunity; the funds necessary will be forthcoming.

A second avenue of progress will be in the scientific understanding of what constitutes and sustains human learning, and what can be done in the way of more effective teaching. The scientific study of the processes of learning and teaching have already brought a new phase of technology into being in the teaching-learning machines. Schools are being designed more functionally also, with an eye to experimentation with new modes of teaching and learning.

Within the curriculum at all levels, from primary grades through college and university, it can safely be predicted that there will be increasing opportunity for students to study independently in laboratory and library. The emphasis will be on learning how to learn, how to assess information, how to establish inferences, and how to judge critically. Less and less time will be spent in passing out to students, by textbook and lecture, what is thought of as subject matter. Subject matter will also gradually lose its sectarian quality, its specialization in exclusive compartments of mathematics, physics, and so on. The mathematical language of science will be evident in the study of all sciences—physical, biological, and social. Ideas of aesthetics will be found in the study of language and industrial arts, as much as in the fine arts.

Programs in physical education and recreation already are well-advanced,

137

though still too much under the shadow of varsity sports. It is more difficult to be optimistic about the co-curricular programs; student newspapers, clubs, and other organizations continue to be afterthoughts. Vocational education will continually be infused with new life, because of the evident need society has for technicians. Vocational training cannot remain the preparation of semiskilled workers for factories, farms, and offices. There are now and will be too many "service" occupations for which training is demanded. The preparation of highly paid technical specialists will attract able young people to the vocational-technical programs.

The services of education specialists, such as guidance-counselor personnel, remedial reading teachers, and others clearly will be made increasingly available. Schools such as those in blighted urban areas will receive special assistance as they have not in the past. The needs of small rural schools, from "programmed learning" services through teaching-learning machines, as substitutes for the more adequate programs of larger schools, will be fulfilled.

Administrators as well as teachers will be better prepared. For the administrators, larger amounts of up-to-date behavior science will be included in their professional preparation, dictated by demands for better informed school leadership and by the fact that school systems will engage technical specialists to assist administrators with records, architectural problems, and questions of finance.

For the Promethean humanist, the curricular changes will be most heartening. He cannot but be delighted with the prospect of new emphasis on learning how to learn, and on inquiry by students. He cannot but be pleased also with the de-emphasizing of authoritarian relationships between teachers and students and teachers and administrators. For all this betokens more adventure in learning, more genuine education.

BIBLIOGRAPHY

1. AIKIN, WILFORD M., *The Story of the Eight-Year Study*. New York: Harper & Row, Publishers, 1942.
2. BAGLEY, WILLIAM C., *The Educative Process*. New York: The Macmillan Co., 1905.
3. BELL, HOWARD M., *Youth Tell Their Story*. Washington, D.C.: American Council on Education, 1938.
4. BESTOR, ARTHUR E., *Educational Wastelands*. Urbana: University of Illinois Press, 1953.
5. BORROWMAN, MERLE L., *The Liberal and the Technical in Teacher Education*. New York: Bureau of Publications, Teachers College, Columbia University, 1956.
6. BRUBACHER, JOHN S., "The Evolution of Professional Education," *Education for the Professions*, Sixty-first Yearbook of the National Society for the Study of Education, Part II, Nelson B. Henry, ed. Chicago: University of Chicago Press, 1962.

7. BRUBACHER, JOHN S. and WILLIS RUDY, *Higher Education in Transition*. New York: Harper & Row, Publishers, 1958.

8. BUTTS, R. FREEMAN and LAWRENCE A. CREMIN, *A History of Education in American Culture*. New York: Holt, Rinehart & Winston, Inc., 1953.

9. COUNTS, GEORGE S., *Dare the Schools Build a New Social Order?* New York: The John Day Company, Inc., 1932.

10. CREMIN, LAWRENCE A., *The American Common School*. New York: Bureau of Publications, Teachers College, Columbia University, 1951.

11. ———, ed., *The Republic and the School: Horace Mann on the Education of Free Men*. New York: Bureau of Publications, Teachers College, Columbia University, 1959.

12. ———, *The Transformation of the School*. New York: Alfred A. Knopf, Inc., 1961.

13. CUBBERLEY, ELLWOOD P., *Public Education in the United States*. Boston: Houghton Mifflin Company, 1934.

14. DEWEY, JOHN, *Democracy and Education*. New York: The Macmillan Company, 1916.

15. ———, *The School and Society*. Chicago: University of Chicago Press, 1900.

16. Educational Policies Commission, National Education Association, *Education for All American Youth*. Washington, D.C.: Educational Policies Commission, 1944.

17. ———, *Education and Economic Well-Being in American Democracy*. Washington, D.C.: Educational Policies Commission, 1940.

18. ———, *The Education of Free Men in American Democracy*. Washington, D.C.: Educational Policies Commission, 1941.

19. ———, *The Purposes of Education in American Democracy*. Washington, D.C.: Educational Policies Commission, 1938.

20. ———, *The Unique Function of Education in American Democracy*. Washington, D.C.: National Education Association of the United States, 1937.

21. FOERSTER, NORMAN, *The Future of the Liberal College*. New York: Appleton-Century-Crofts, Inc., 1938.

22. ———, *The Humanities and the Common Man*. Chapel Hill: University of North Carolina Press, 1946.

23. HENRY, NELSON B., *Adapting the Secondary School to the Needs of Youth*, The Fifty-second Yearbook of the National Society for the Study of Education, Part I. Chicago: University of Chicago Press, 1953.

24. ———, *Education for the Professions*, The Sixty-first Yearbook of the National Society for the Study of Education. Chicago: University of Chicago Press, 1962.

25. ———, ed., *General Education*, The Fifty-first Yearbook of the National Society for the Study of Education, Part I. Chicago: University of Chicago Press, 1952.

26. HENRY, NELSON B., *Personnel Services in Education,* The Fifty-eighth Yearbook of the National Society for the Study of Education. Chicago: University of Chicago Press, 1959.

27. ———, *Rethinking Science Education,* The Fifty-ninth Yearbook of the National Society for the Study of Education. Chicago: University of Chicago Press, 1960.

28. ———, *Social Studies in the Elementary School,* The Fifty-sixth Yearbook of the National Society for the Study of Education, Part II. Chicago: University of Chicago Press, 1957.

29. HUTCHINS, ROBERT M., *The Higher Learning in America.* New Haven: Yale University Press, 1936.

30. KILPATRICK, WILLIAM H., ed., *The Educational Frontier.* New York: Appleton-Century-Crofts, Inc., 1933.

31. ———, "The Project Method," *Teachers College Record,* XIX, No. 4 (1918), 319-335.

32. KILPATRICK, WILLIAM H., WILLIAM C. BAGLEY, FREDERICK G. BONSER, and JAMES H. HOSIC, "Dangers and Difficulties of the Project Method and How to Overcome Them—A Symposium," *Teachers College Record,* XXII, No. 4 (1921), 283-321.

33. KNIGHT, EDGAR W. and CLIFTON L. HALL, *Readings in American Educational History.* New York: Appleton-Century-Crofts, Inc., 1951.

34. LAMAR, JOHNSON B., "Purposes and Plan of the Yearbook," *The Public Junior College.* The Fifty-fifth Yearbook of the National Society for the Study of Education, Part I, Nelson B. Henry, ed. Chicago: University of Chicago Press, 1956.

35. LIEBERMAN, MYRON, *Education as a Profession.* Englewood Cliffs, N.J.: Prentice-Hall, Inc., 1956.

36. LINDSEY, MARGARET, ed., *New Horizons for the Teaching Profession.* Washington, D.C.: National Commission on Teacher Education and Professional Standards, National Education Association, 1961.

37. MACLEAN, MALCOLM and DAN W. DODSON, "Educational Needs Emerging from the Changing Demands of Society," *The Public Junior College.* The Fifty-fifth Yearbook of the National Society for the Study of Education, Part I, Nelson B. Henry, ed. Chicago: University of Chicago Press, 1956.

38. MCMURRY, CHARLES A., *The Elements of General Method.* Bloomington, Ill.: Public-School Publishing Company, 1892.

39. ———, *The Method of the Recitation.* Bloomington, Ill.: Public-School Publishing Company, 1897.

40. MONROE, WALTER S., *Teacher-Learning Theory and Teacher Education, 1890-1950.* Urbana: University of Illinois Press, 1952.

41. National Education Association of the United States, *Cardinal Principles of Secondary Education,* Bureau of Education, Bulletin No. 35, 1918.

42. ———, *Implications of Social-Economic Goals.* Washington, D.C.: National Education Association of the United States, 1937.

43. ———, *Report of the Committee on College Entrance Requirements.* Chicago: University of Chicago Press, 1899.

44. National Education Association of the United States, *Report of the Committee of Fifteen on Elementary Education*. New York: American Book Company, 1895.

45. ———, *Report of the Committee of Ten on Secondary School Studies*. Washington, D.C.: Government Printing Office, 1893.

46. PAGE, DAVID P., *Theory and Practice of Teaching*. Syracuse, N.Y.: Hall and Dickson, 1847.

47. RICKOVER, HYMAN G., *Education and Freedom*. New York: E. P. Dutton & Co., Inc., 1959.

48. "Progress of Reform in the Boston Schools," *Common School Journal*, VIII, No. 5 (1846).

49. RUGG, HAROLD and ANN SHUMAKER, *The Child-Centered School*. New York: Harcourt, Brace & World, Inc., 1928.

50. SCHMIDT, GEORGE P., *The Liberal Arts College*. New Brunswick, N.J.: Rutgers University Press, 1957.

51. SMITH, NILA B., *American Reading Instruction*. New York: Silver Burdett Company, 1934.

52. TANNENBAUM, ABRAHAM J., "History of Interest in the Gifted," *Education for the Gifted*, The Fifty-seventh Yearbook of the National Society for the Study of Education, Part II, Nelson B. Henry, ed. Chicago: University of Chicago Press, 1958.

53. THAYER, V. T., *The Passing of the Recitation*. Boston: D. C. Heath & Company, 1928.

54. ———, *The Role of the School in American Society*. New York: Dodd, Mead & Co., 1960.

55. "Twenty-five Years of Educational Research," *Review of Educational Research*, XXVI, No. 3 (1956).

56. VEBLEN, THORSTEIN, *The Higher Learning in America*. New York: B. W. Huebsch, 1918.

57. WALLIN, J. E., *The Education of Handicapped Children*. Boston: Houghton Mifflin Company, 1924.

58. WESLEY, EDGAR B., *NEA: The First Hundred Years*. New York: Harper & Row, Publishers, 1957.

59. WHIPPLE, GUY M., ed., *The Foundations and Technique of Curriculum-Construction*, The Twenty-sixth Yearbook of the National Society for the Study of Education, Part II, Bloomington, Ill.: Public-School Publishing Company, 1930.

60. WHITE, EMERSON E., *The Elements of Pedagogy*. New York: American Book Company, 1886.

61. ———, *School Management*. New York: American Book Company, 1893.

62. WRIGHT, ARTHUR D. and GEORGE E. GARDNER, *Hall's Lectures on School-Keeping*. Hanover, N.H.: The Dartmouth Press, 1929.

143

INDEX

148